THE TEXAS HILL COUNTRY
Cookbook

A TASTE OF PROVENCE

Chef Scott Cohen and Marian Betancourt
Photography by Ron Manville

ThreeForks™

GUILFORD, CONNECTICUT
HELENA, MONTANA

AN IMPRINT OF THE GLOBE PEQUOT PRESS

ThreeForks is a trademark of Morris Book Publishing, LLC.

Photos © Ron Manville, except pp. 44, 154 © Becker Vineyards and p. 132 © Alicia Stoltz
Text design by Nancy Freeborn

Library of Congress Cataloging-in-Publication Data is available.
ISBN 978-0-7627-4375-9

Manufactured in China
First Edition/First Printing

This is for my wife, Jamie, and our children, Daniel, Samantha, and James;
to everyone in our families, and to the memory of my father, Leonard Cohen,
and my father-in-law, James Brown, whose loving spirits are with us always.

S.C.

CONTENTS

THE FRESHEST SALADS AND A FEW SANDWICHES

THE FUN OF FISH

MEAT, GAME, AND POULTRY

VEGETABLES AND SIDE DISHES

DESSERTS

FROM THE CHEF'S PANTRY

ACKNOWLEDGMENTS

A chef is nothing without his kitchen staff, and I appreciate them all, especially Isaac Cantu, executive sous chef, who has been with me from my first day in San Antonio; sous chefs Wayne Brooks, Stevie Paprocki, Chris Cook, Andy Galvan, Jose Yanez, and former sous chef Eric Nelson. Special thanks to Mark Chapman, who was our pastry chef when this book began and who worked with me in New York.

The people who manage the overall kitchen and dining room operations are much appreciated: food and beverage director Philippe Wilhelm, who kept me sane and focused during the time we wrote this book; Philippe Placé, Las Canarias' general manager and the best maître d' I have ever worked with; and Luciano Ciorciari, Pesca on the River's general manager, who helped make it the best fish restaurant in Texas.

I owe gratitude and thanks to many people who have contributed to my professional experience in Texas: Rusty Wallace, general manager of Omni's La Mansion del Rio and Watermark Hotel and Spa; Fernando Salazar, vice president of food and beverage; and to Bob Rowling, owner of Omni Hotels, for their support and enthusiasm for this book; also David Lurie, Jack Hebden, Jon Sakshaug, Manny Garcia-Rubio, Eileen Read, Adilya Kleinpeter, Michael Bazaar, and Beth Smith. Thanks also to past president of the hotels Henry Feldman and past owner Pat Kennedy, both of whom shared my passion for the restaurants.

My career really began in New York; where the late Andre Gaillard, with whom I worked at La Reserve, put the "chef" into me. Thanks and gratitude go to his memory. Thanks to Daniel Boulud, the extraordinary chef and restaurateur who urged me to go to Provence, which changed my life as a chef. I am indebted to the James Beard Foundation, especially to Jacques Pepin, and to its late founder, Peter Kump. Chef Jean-Yves Pique, former president of Vatel, also helped to mold me as a chef.

A big helping of gratitude and love goes to Jeanne Wilensky, public relations consultant in New York and still my friend, who taught me that it's not how many times your name appears in the media; it's how many people you influence. And to Barbara Lazeroff, whose positive energy and presence made me want to work harder. Thanks to Brian Miller, former restaurant critic at the *New York Times*, who put me on the culinary map; to the San Antonio food press, John Griffin, Bonnie Walker, Karen Haram, Pat Mozersky, and Ron Bechtol; and to Sarah Cocoran, Jane Satel, and

Scott Jones, executive editor of *Southern Living,* who help keep my career in the public eye in San Antonio.

I owe a great deal to Graham Kerr because I still vividly remember sitting in front of the TV at age 5 eating a tuna sandwich on white bread and being completely entranced by *The Galloping Gourmet.* I'm positive he put me on the road I'm on today.

When I arrived in San Antonio, Robert Maggiani of the Texas Department of Agriculture introduced me to the farmers of the Texas Hill Country and I am forever in his debt. Also thanks to Jeanne Strickland for showing me the area's great orchards.

Special thanks go to my coauthor, Marian Betancourt, for her creative vision and persistence with this book. Thanks also to Wolfgang Puck, with whom I worked at The Mansion on Turtle Creek in Dallas when I was starting out and where I met my wife. I am grateful to my mother, Paulette Cohen, and my mother-in-law, Annette Brown, for their support.

And most of all, my love and gratitude goes to Jamie, my wife of 20 years, who has coped with the stresses that a chef's life puts on a family. She has kept me strong and our kids safe, and I can't express how grateful I am.

S.C.

Thanks to Nancy Love, the kind of agent all writers want because she never gives up on a good idea; to Megan Hiller and Heather Carreiro at Globe Pequot, for seeing the value in this food and this book; to designer Nancy Freeborn, for making the book so elegant; to Joan Brunskill, my editor at Associated Press Features for many years, for encouraging my early forays into food writing; to Elaine Khosrova, senior editor at *Santé* magazine, for always finding space for my culinary enthusiasms; and to Kelly Garland of Geiger and Associates, for introducing me to San Antonio and the Texas Hill Country. And, of course, thanks to chef extraordinaire Scott Cohen, whose enthusiasm for using locally grown food is so important to the people who eat in his restaurants.

M.B.

PREFACE

When I began cooking in San Antonio and discovered that everything I needed was within a twenty-minute drive, I thought I had died and gone to heaven—or at least back to the South of France, where I had trained many years ago. We have game ranches, produce farms, apple orchards, vineyards, and artisan cheese makers. Lavender fields, herb farms, pecans, and peaches are all around us. Olive growers are producing another kind of oil in Texas—something to rival the Mediterranean. The agricultural abundance of the Texas Hill Country is on a par with Provence and has inspired some of the best cooking in my twenty-year career. It's as if everything I learned and already knew came together here.

My creativity and passion for cooking thrive in a part of the country that is fast becoming a culinary hot spot. Stories about the Texas Hill Country, located in the region around the major metropolitan areas of Austin and San Antonio, appear more and more frequently in national food and travel magazines and newspapers. The local farmers and artisans who supply my kitchens at Las Canarias and Pesca on the River are all part of my menu. My wife's Texas farm family also inspired my love of the land here. They devoted four acres to vegetables for family, friends, and their church. This is where I learned about planting and harvesting, and that it's best to wear gloves when picking okra. They taught me some of the same lessons I learned in the South of France, where I discovered how the "Cuisine of the Sun" respects the seasons, sustains the land, and uses food in the simplest and most natural way. In other words, it's modern Provençal cooking with a decidedly Texas twist. I like to call my cooking Tex-Sun.

Every month at Las Canarias and Pesca on the River, our tasting menus highlight local products, such as tomatoes, peaches, onions, and baby greens. But this is not another back-to-the-land book. That was done years ago. Nor is it a typical Texas barbecue or Tex-Mex book, of which there are many. This is a book about fine cuisine, which I believe home cooks can achieve using fresh, locally grown foods prepared with classic techniques and served with style. I've developed these dishes at the restaurants over the years. Some are old favorites, and some are new. All are inspired by the food of this great region.

I hope *The Texas Hill Country Cookbook* will inspire you to become more aware of how foods naturally complement each other in taste and texture. Let this book help you plan meals, find the best ingredients, hone your technique, and go off on your own creative culinary adventures. Some recipes are simple and easy, and some are more challenging. If you enjoy spending time in the garden or at the market and in the kitchen, savoring the tastes, textures, sights, and fragrances of fresh foods, then this book is for you.

You'll find some tips to help transform any dish with technique, better or un-expected ingredients, creative presentation—or all of the above. There are recipes and advice on techniques for sauces and demi-glaces, so important to finishing a dish perfectly. For example, a slight variation in viscosity, seasoning, or cooking time can mean the difference between an average and a superlative sauce. People in my cook-ing classes at San Antonio's Central Market and diners at the restaurants tell me how their own cooking was transformed when they followed my simple suggestions.

Fabulous food tastes, smells, and looks so good, that you remember the pleasure for a long time. It is a hint of fresh mint in a chilled snap pea soup. It is making lamb extraordinary with a wine and lavender jus. It is the tangy sweetness of a just-picked tomato.

The Texas Hill Country Cookbook is a window into Texas Hill Country and why it is on the culinary map. Throughout the book, you'll find stories about some of these food producers. Come and visit soon.

SCOTT COHEN

INTRODUCTION

"Provence is a dead ringer for Hill Country," wrote Patricia Sharpe, in *Texas Monthly* in 2004. "Until recently, though, the resemblance stopped with the terrain. The singular terroir of Provence—the character of the land that manifests itself in the region's wine, olives and olive oil, herbs, lavender, goat cheese, lamb, and honey—had no homegrown counterpart. But all that has changed in the past decade, as a gaggle of entrepreneurs—some starry-eyed, some sharp-eyed—has started transforming the local landscape."

In fact, this rebirth that Sharpe describes has encouraged agricultural tourism. People come to Texas Hill Country to follow the lavender trails, visit the wineries, and pick the peaches. Our annual Poteet Strawberry Festival is the biggest in the country. Cora Lamar of Oak Hill Farms, who won the 2006 prize for the finest strawberries, said recently that she turned down a request for her strawberries from Thomas Keller's exclusive Per Se restaurant in New York, because she did not want to ship them that far, fearing they would not be as tasty after a long trip. "I'm just a country girl," she said, acknowledging that her farm doesn't even have a Web site.

The Hill Country, roughly between Austin and San Antonio, was settled by German immigrants in 1846, and this heritage is honored at the annual Founder's Day Festival, sponsored by the Gillespie County Historical Society. Today Gillespie County tops the list of the Southwest's ten best rural counties in which to live. The area was always the site of produce, from kitchen gardens to small farms. In the 1850s, the landscape architect Frederick Law Olmsted was traveling through Texas by horseback and had grown tired of the greasy fried meat he found in most of the West. But he made a note in his journal about the German kitchen gardens where he got "two dishes of vegetables, salad, compote of peaches . . . wheat bread from the loaf, and beautiful and sweet butter."

The Hill Country was always a fine agricultural area, with its sandy loam, good drainage, and mild climate, but much of the land was given over to cattle. When that business declined in the 1970s and 1980s, land was sold off as smaller cattle "ranchettes," to people leaving the cattle or oil business, who discovered they could make a living by creating a market for high-value crops such as tomatoes, strawberries, and other fruits and vegetables. Some even began growing things that experts said would not grow in Hill Country.

Baxter and Carol Adams proved the experts wrong when they began their Love Creek Farm orchards with dwarf apple trees in the 1980s. Baxter Adams was a geologist in Houston, and when the oil business dried up, he and Carol moved to Medina, a Hill Country town of 200 people. They thought the land might be suitable for raising dwarf apple trees. Despite what the experts told them, they learned of a place in Romania with the same characteristics and climate where dwarf apple trees were successfully grown. So after consulting with Dr. Stephan Sheric, who heads the Romanian fruit and nut industry, they forged ahead. (Dr. Sheric still comes to Medina every year to see how the apples are doing.)

The one hundred dwarf trees at Love Creek grow the sweetest apples ever tasted because they are allowed to ripen on the tree—rather than be picked before their prime and artificially ripened—so they contain 20 percent more sugar. When the first apple crop was ready, Baxter and Carol invited the whole town to come and pick some apples and try them out. If everybody in town came with some of their friends, they figured, they'd have about 300 people at the apple party. Of course, 3,000 showed up, and soon Medina needed a community development corporation to handle the apple seekers. At Love Creek, a few apple pies were made each day in a tiny oven, but the demand increased until they were making many more, and the pies were featured on national television on the Food Network. Since then, the last Friday in July is the annual Great Hill Country Apple Picking.

Another story of bucking conventional wisdom involves Texas Sweet onions, the forerunners of Georgia's Vidalia onions. These are sweet enough to eat like an apple. Known as Texas 1015 onions for the suggested planting date of October 15, they are often called million dollar babies because of the cost it allegedly took their creator, Dr. Leonard Pike, professor at Texas A&M University, to develop them. We feature these onions in many parts of our menus.

Cora and Bob Lamar, with their son Chris, grow 150 acres of tomatoes, squash, strawberries, blackberries, and other produce on their Oak Hill Farm in Poteet, which was a cattle ranch until the 1980s. When Cora calls me in June and says, "I got maters," I drop everything, hop into my Jeep, and head out to this wonderful farm to pick my own from a variety of red and yellow tomatoes, cherry, teardrop, all kinds. They are fabulous in our chilled gazpacho, or tossed with freshly made cavatelli.

In 2006, the Lamars, originally from Austin, were the grand champions in the Poteet Strawberry Festival, which features not only the wonderful strawberries of the area but also music and all kinds of family fun and games. The first festival was held in 1948, and Henry and Ida Mumme, the city's founders, might be flabbergasted to see how their original kitchen garden has grown. How my kitchen staff loves to make strawberry shortcake and chilled strawberry soup with crunchy meringue, or use them in a baby spinach salad with toasted almonds, shaved red onions, and poppy seed vinaigrette.

Dewberries, native to central Texas, also grow in abundance in Poteet. They have a terrific sweet/tart flavor with a musky "wildness." We've used them in salads, in a dewberry-lemon emulsion for grilled shrimp, and as a chilled dessert soup.

Hill Country peaches are rarely talked about outside the state, because we don't want to pick them before their time and ship them all around the globe. Gillespie County in Hill Country supplies a third of the state's peaches, and we pick them right from the tree. You'll enjoy making our peach cobbler with them.

And the wine! Texas Hill Country wines are winning prizes in international competitions because our sandy, well-drained soil, warm sunny days, cool nights, low humidity, and constant air flow are similar to regions in France. Early in our history, mustang grapes grew wild along the rivers and streams of Texas, and in the 1600s, Spanish missionaries established vineyards in what is today El Paso. In the 1800s, European immigrants planted cuttings in Hill Country that they had brought from home. By 1900 there were more than 25 wineries in Texas, but Prohibition ended wine making until the resurgence of wine popularity in the United States. Now there are nearly fifty wineries in the state, with the largest portion in Hill Country. We serve many of these wines in our restaurants, including some of the best from Becker Vineyards and Fall Creek Vineyards.

Dr. Richard Becker and his wife, Bunny, grow several varietals, including syrah, chardonnay, and merlot. Their winery is a reproduction of a German stone barn and is surrounded by grazing horses, peach orchards, and fields of lavender, which have become synonymous with the rolling hills of central Texas, just as they are in the hills of Provence.

Several different types of lavender bloom from early May through June, when tourists flock to the area. It's widely known that lavender is used in soaps and per-fumes, but few know how often it is used in cooking—and how to use it. The heat of Texas intensifies the oil in the plant, which can be used in both sweet and savory dishes. We use it to make honey lavender ice cream, and it is especially delicious in the jus of roasted lamb.

Olive oil is still a blip on the Texas screen, but we have six growers producing oil. So far a grower in Wimberly has the only olive press, but the Department of Agri-culture is helping the growers fund a rolling press, so it can circulate to all the growers at harvesttime.

We have mushrooms, potatoes, honey, and artisan cheese makers. One day we may call this Little Provence. It's a chef's paradise, so you can see why I love cooking in the midst of all this abundance.

If you cannot cultivate relationships with local farmers and artisans, the way I can, look for the best seasonal ingredients at farmers' markets and some local stores. Farmers' markets are more and more popular, especially in large metropolitan areas. Products from regional farms are picked in the morning and sold the same day. The food travels only 50 or 100 miles from the farm. Here in Texas, we have such markets in most of our cities. In Texas Hill Country, there are fifty or sixty farmers' markets, usually held once a week in the small towns. In addition to seasonal fruits and vegetables, these markets often carry artisan products, such as cheeses and breads, and "yard eggs," from local farms that allow their chickens to run in the yard, rather than stay cooped up in small cages for their entire lives.

Most produce in this country is mass produced on factory farms, harvested before its time, and artificially ripened. On the three- or four-day journey from California to New York, tomatoes may be gassed inside the truck, after first sitting in a warehouse in California, then in the truck and at wholesale centers in New York, and who knows how many days in the supermarket before it gets to your kitchen. The tomatoes are weeks old, mealy, mushy, flavorless, and lacking in the nutrients they produced while they were growing. Avoid such food at all costs. The "maters" I get from Oak Hill Farms have tender skin and juice that gushes forth like the best Texas oil well.

When there is no farmers' market, shop where local produce is available. Some supermarkets now put signs over the produce to indicate which is organic, local, or conventional. Ask your vendors where they get their food and how often it arrives. Talk to chefs at your favorite restaurants and ask where they get their produce. More and more of them are using local farms. Look for bright colors, fresh aroma, and crisp texture. A string bean should "snap," and leafy greens should be perky. A tomato should have tender skin and be juicy. Some of those pale pink tomatoes in the supermarket don't have a drop of juice in them. As Cora Lamar knows, shipping her berries a long distance might mean less than perfection.

We are living in an exciting era of change about the way we eat, coming full circle. After industrialization removed us from the front line of food, the pendulum is swinging back: We now want to experience real food that grows nearby.

Remember that a fabulous meal begins with fabulous ingredients.

APPETIZERS

With the growing popularity of tapas and mezze, the Mediterranean style of "small plates," appetizers are taking on a new life. Some restaurant guests order several appetizers rather than the traditional appetizer followed by the entree and dessert. Appetizers can also be used to serve an entire dinner party, and it's a fun way to experience a lot of different tastes to satisfy diverse palettes. For example, the pissaladière can be cut into small wedges and passed around. The buffalo carpaccio is another appetizer that can be shared. Some of these recipes, such as the red beet risotto, can also be used as a side dish.

When you do serve an appetizer in the traditional way, it sets you up for the next course, so it's important to plan it along with the full meal in mind.

ROASTED RED BEET RISOTTO
with Cremini Mushrooms and Shaved Parmesan

The flavor of the roasted beets and the beautiful red color from the beet stock add to the unique presentation of this dish. The creminis have a delicate and mild taste, which doesn't overpower the beets. The slow process of gradually stirring liquid into risotto is well worth the effort, for the tender arborio rice picks up the earthy flavors of the mushrooms and Parmesan, which balance the sweetness of the beets. This dish is easier to make than it sounds because you can roast the beets, make the stock, and sauté the mushrooms in advance. You can precook the risotto a day before serving by leaving part of the process unfinished. After adding a cup of stock for the second time, take it off the stove, cool it on a half-sheet pan, and put it in the fridge. Then, to finish the next day, add ¼ cup of the beet stock, continue stirring, and add the Parmesan and butter. This dish can also take on a seasonal flavor by adding another vegetable, such as fresh spring peas.

3 pounds red beets of similar size, cleaned and trimmed of roots and stems

Beet Stock

1 yellow onion, rough chopped

2 carrots, peeled and rough chopped

2 stalks celery, rough chopped

2 cups dry red wine

1 teaspoon whole black peppercorns

1 teaspoon salt

3 parsley stems

1 gallon water

3 pounds roasted and diced beets (from above)

Mushrooms

1 pound cremini mushrooms

2 tablespoons (approximately) olive oil

Risotto

¼ cup olive oil

1 shallot, minced

1 cup arborio rice

¾ cup dry red wine

3–4 cups beet stock

2 tablespoons butter

3 tablespoons Parmesan, shredded (save some cheese to shave for garnish)

½ cup sautéed cremini mushrooms

¼ cup diced roasted red beets

¼ teaspoon salt or to taste

White pepper to taste

Roast the beets: Wrap each beet in tinfoil to prevent too much juice from escaping and place them on a sheet pan in a 350-degree oven until tender, about 40 minutes. Remove foil and allow the beets to cool before peeling them. (Skin should come off easily in your hand.) Dice the beets into ¼×¼-inch cubes and set aside. Save ¼ cup diced beets for garnish later.

Prepare the beet stock: In a large pot over medium-high heat, sweat the onions, carrots, and celery, being careful not to let them color. Add the red wine and allow it to reduce by half. Add the peppercorns, salt, parsley stems, and water. Bring to a boil and lower heat to a simmer; cook for 45 minutes. Strain the stock through a fine-mesh strainer. Once strained, add the diced beets. Puree the mixture with a hand blender right in the pot. The stock should have a deep red color. For every cup of rice, you will need 3 to 4 cups of beet stock in addition to 1 cup of wine, so this large amount of stock will be used up.

Prepare the mushrooms: Clean the mushrooms (can be washed or brushed) and slice them. In a small skillet, sauté the mushrooms in olive oil and set aside.

Prepare the risotto: In a large sauté pan, sweat the shallots in the olive oil. Stir in the rice until it is nicely coated by the oil. Deglaze with red wine and allow it to reduce while constantly stirring. Once reduced by half, add in the beet stock, ½ cup at a time, stirring often and not allowing the rice to get dry. Once the rice has finished cooking in about 15 or 20 minutes, stir in the butter and the Parmesan until they melt. Fold in the diced beets and mushrooms and season with salt and white pepper. The risotto should have a creamy consistency.

To serve: Put a mound of risotto in the center of each large white round plate. Using a potato peeler, shave some more Parmesan on top and serve.

SERVES 4

PREP TIP: When preparing fresh beets, leave some of the stem and root intact so you don't cut into the flesh. This will cause the beet to "bleed" while cooking.

FLAVOR TIP: Parsley stems impart flavor during the cooking process without adding the bitterness you would get from overcooking parsley leaves.

BLACK OLIVE TAPENADE
with Pickled Nopalitos

Olives always take me back to the South of France and the Mediterranean, but in Texas I discovered a perfect match for this wonderful fruit—nopalitos. These are the pickled "pads" of the prickly pear cactus, and they taste a bit like green beans. Prickly pear grows wild and can be harvested by anyone. The "tuna" is the fruit on top of the cactus, and this part is used in drinks. The thorns in the pad must be removed by hand—a tedious job—but the pickled nopalitos have been dethorned. By combining olives and the desert prickly pear, you have a delicious appetizer that pairs extremely well with goat cheese.

Tapenade

2 cups pitted black niçoise olives

¼ cup (approximately) extra virgin olive oil

1 anchovy fillet

1 teaspoon capers

½ cup chopped nopalitos pickles (see Shopping Tip)

1 sprig fresh thyme, chopped

1 teaspoon Xeres or other top quality sherry vinegar

Salt and freshly ground black pepper to taste

2 tablespoons extra virgin olive oil

1 teaspoon dried herbes de Provence

8 ounces young goat cheese

Prepare the tapenade: In a food processor, pulse the olives until coarsely chopped. Add olive oil, anchovy, capers, nopalitos, thyme, vinegar, salt, and pepper, and continue to pulse. You should get the consistency of a loose paste. Remove and reserve in refrigerator.

To serve: Place 1 tablespoon of the tapenade in the center of each of 8 small plates. Drizzle olive oil around the tapenade and sprinkle herbes de Provence around the plate. Serve with assorted soft goat cheeses, about 2 ounces per plate.

SERVES 8

SHOPPING TIPS: Nopalitos pickles are available everywhere in the Southwest, and in Mexican or gourmet stores elsewhere.

There are two types of goat cheese. Soft or young goat cheese is the most widely known, but many people prefer aged goat cheese, which is firm.

BUFFALO CARPACCIO
with Herbed Quinoa, Spicy Tomato Coulis, and Watercress Sauce

Buffalo—or bison—are not raised in Texas, so we get ours from Colorado. This delicious and tender meat has much less fat than beef, so it's important not to cook it through or it will dry out. Carpaccio is usually raw, but in this recipe, we sear the whole piece of tenderloin all around the outside for only 10 to 15 seconds to provide a crisp edge to the slices. Serve this with herbed quinoa, spicy tomato coulis, and watercress sauce. The red and green sauces with the creamy quinoa make a beautiful presentation. All the components can be prepared ahead of time and assembled just before serving.

1 6-ounce piece of buffalo tenderloin
Salt and black pepper for presear seasoning
1 tablespoon herbes de Provence
1 teaspoon or less olive oil
½ cup spicy tomato coulis (see recipe page 137)

½ cup watercress sauce (see recipe page 138)
1 cup herbed quinoa (see recipe page 113)

8 watercress leaves for garnish

Prepare the carpaccio: Season the buffalo tenderloin with salt and pepper, then roll it in the herbes de Provence. Using a pastry brush, coat a 6-inch omelet pan with the oil and heat the pan until smoking hot. Over very high heat, sear the outside of the tenderloin. Don't let the meat cook; 10 to 15 seconds a side will do. Let the seared meat cool thoroughly before putting it into the freezer until it is very cold but not frozen (about an hour) to make slicing easier. Using a very sharp knife, slice the tenderloin as thinly as possible, and place these circular slices between two sheets of waxed paper or plastic wrap. Lightly tap them (don't pound too hard) so the circles become paper thin. Return to the freezer for about 20 minutes. Remove one of the sheets of paper and flip the carpaccio over onto an 8- or 10-inch plate, then remove the other sheet of paper.

To serve: Each plate should have 3–4 slices. Using spoons, lightly drizzle some spicy tomato coulis and some watercress sauce around the carpaccio. Also using a spoon, shape a small amount of quinoa for the center of the carpaccio. Garnish with two watercress leaves.
Serve chilled.

SERVES 4

PISSALADIÈRE
with Texas Goat Cheese

This is my easy version of a Provençal pizza that I make with Mediterranean olives, truffle oil, Texas 1015 onions, and Texas goat cheese. This is a single-serving pizza, about 5 inches in diameter. Make this up in batches and keep it in the freezer to use as a last-minute party canapé. It's also a great snack, and kids love it.

Sauce

1 tablespoon tapenade (store bought is fine, or use recipe on page 10)

4 drops garlic oil

½ teaspoon herbes de Provence

Pissaladière

1 package ready-made croissant dough

½ Texas 1015 (or other) sweet onion, sliced and caramelized

½ tablespoon soft goat cheese

3 kalamata olives cut in half

2 teaspoons grated Parmesan cheese

1 pinch chopped fresh flat-leaf parsley

1 pinch herbes de Provence

1 teaspoon white truffle oil

Prepare the sauce: In a small bowl, mix tapenade, garlic oil, and herbes de Provence and set aside.

Prepare the pizza: Cut croissant dough with a 5-inch fluted pie cutter. Spread thin layer of the tapenade sauce on the dough, then make a second layer of the caramelized onions. Break up goat cheese, place on top. Sprinkle with olive pieces. Bake on a sheet pan in a 400-degree oven for 6 to 7 minutes until crust is golden brown.

To serve: Place pizza on a large dinner plate and sprinkle Parmesan, parsley, and herbes de Provence around it. Sprinkle with white truffle oil and cut into fours.

SERVES 1

SHOPPING TIP: Sheets of ready-made croissant dough can be found in the freezer section of fine food stores. There's enough in the package to make 4 of the above recipe.

PREP TIP: If you keep a batch of these pizzas in the freezer, just pop one into the oven the same way you would with a fresh pizza. In fact, the frozen ones seem to come out even crispier.

CHILE-SPIKED MEXICAN SHRIMP
with Cilantro and Huitlacoche Vinaigrette

Not only is this delicious, but the black sauce, pink shrimp, and green garnish make a beautiful presentation on a white or glass plate. I created this dish for a black tie dinner at the San Antonio Food and Wine Festival, and it was later published in *Food Arts* magazine. I like to use wild (not farmed) Mexican shrimp from the Gulf because they are sweeter than other shrimp. The hot peppers in this recipe are also specialties from Mexico and are the best to use. However, if you cannot find all of them in your area, then I've included a way to use ready-made high-quality chile powder. The shrimp will be coated in a spicy mix of these powders and bread crumbs that can also be used on other fried fish and some meats, such as rack of lamb. Cilantro and the spicy huitlacoche vinaigrette are great complements to the sweet shrimp.

Bread Coating

1 cup panko bread crumbs

½ dried guajillo pepper

½ dried pasilla pepper

½ dried chile Pequin

¼ dried ancho chile pepper

¼ dried cayenne pepper

(Note: Find as many as you can of the above peppers. If you can't, use a total of 1 tablespoon of good-quality chile powder.)

1 tablespoon melted butter (lightly browned)

1 tablespoon washed and finely chopped fresh flat-leaf parsley

Olive oil if needed for consistency of bread mixture

¼ teaspoon salt or to taste

Shrimp

12 shrimp, U/12 or 16/20 size

Salt for seasoning

4 tablespoons huitlacoche vinaigrette (see recipe page 144)

Few sprigs of fresh cilantro

Chile oil (see page 143)

Reserved bread coating

Prepare the bread coating: Seed and dry the peppers (see Prep Tip) and grind them into a powder using a spice grinder. (Save a bit of the spice mix to dust on the plate later.) Mix the powder with the bread crumbs in a food processor. Pulse in melted butter until crumbs are soft and slightly sticky. If necessary, add some olive oil to avoid clumps in the mixture. Turn off processor and mix in parsley by hand.

Prepare the shrimp. Preheat oven to 350 degrees. Clean, devein, and butterfly the shrimp. Pat them dry with paper towel. Season with salt and toss them in the crumb mixture until they are totally covered. Bake them on a sheet pan for about 10 to 12 minutes or until done. (Don't put any oil on the sheet pan.)

To serve: Arrange 3 shrimp on each of 4 individual white or glass oval plates with butterfly side up and tails facing toward the edge of the plate. Put approximately 1 tablespoon of the huitlacoche vinaigrette in the middle of each plate. Garnish the vinaigrette with sprigs of micro cilantro and drizzle the plate with chile oil. Sprinkle some of the reserved spice powder over the dish.

SERVES 4

SHOPPING TIP: Shrimp are organized into categories based on size, from the colossal (10 or fewer per pound) to the small (36 to 45 per pound). The size used here, U/12 (up to 12 per pound), are called jumbo; 16/20 are extra large.

PREP TIP: To dry peppers, seed them and put them on a sheet pan in a 250-degree oven for about an hour.

BAY SCALLOP CEVICHE
with Texas Ruby Red Grapefruit and Roasted Peppers

Texas grapefruit smells like sunshine. It is sweeter than most other types and not quite so acidic. In this recipe the sweet tang of the grapefruit rounds out the richness of the scallops. I made this dish at a James Beard Foundation fund-raising golf event (where I came in second) in Williamsburg, Virginia, and food writer Alan Richman declared it one of the best dishes of the day. There are hundreds of versions of ceviche, and fish can be marinated in almost any citrus. But the special flavors of the grapefruit zest, roasted peppers, and baby or micro herbs give this dish an elegance of flavor. I like the baby organic herbs, including mint and amaranth, which has a delicate and slightly sweet flavor, from Texas Blue Bonnet Farm for garnish. Their delicate but pungent flavors survived my flight to Williamsburg when I carried them with me in a flat of 3-inch pots.

Grapefruit
3 fresh Ruby Red grapefruits, segmented,
    then squeezed for juice

Peppers
1 yellow pepper
1 red pepper
1 poblano pepper

Ceviche
2 pounds fresh bay scallops
¼–½ cup fresh Texas Ruby Red (or other
    red grapefruit) juice (see Shopping Tip)
¼ cup fresh Mexican (or other) lime juice
¼ cup fresh lemon juice
¼ cup fresh orange juice
1 tablespoon extra virgin olive oil
2 tablespoons chopped fresh cilantro
1 tablespoon chopped fresh flat-leaf parsley
¼ cup good French cognac
Salt and freshly ground black pepper
Dash of cayenne pepper

1 small bunch micro cilantro, chiffonade
1 small bunch amaranth, chiffonade
1 small bunch mint (optional), chiffonade
Candied grapefruit zest (see recipe page 151)

SHOPPING TIP: Fresh Texas grapefruit is available from November to April. Red grapefruit is also grown in California and Florida, but Texas Ruby Reds are best for this dish. They have a thin skin, give more juices, and have fewer seeds.

Prepare the grapefruit: With a sharp knife, segment three grapefruit. Set the segments aside for plating later and remove the zest for garnish. Squeeze out the juice for the ceviche marinade.

Prepare the peppers: Using long tongs, roast the peppers over a high open flame on the stove. (Or you can put the peppers under the broiler.) When the skin is burned black on all sides, put the peppers in a bowl and cover with plastic wrap. Let them sit for at least 5 minutes so the skin will be easy to remove. Cut the peppers in half, remove the seeds and pith, and scrape off the skin with your fingers or a sharp knife. Dice the peppers very small and mix together. You should have about 1 cup.

Prepare the ceviche: In a large bowl, mix together the peppers, scallops, fruit juices, olive oil, cilantro, parsley, cognac, salt and pepper, and cayenne. Marinate for 6 hours in the refrigerator. Citrus continues to "cook" the fish, and the texture of the scallops will change with each day (and so will the flavor). You can keep it up to 3 days.

To serve: Arrange ceviche on a plate and top with candied grapefruit zest and sprig of baby herbs. This also looks great in a martini or margarita glass.

SERVES 8

CRISPY CALAMARI
with Red Pepper Jalapeño Vinegar and Smoky Tomato Sauce

The two most popular dipping sauces at the restaurants are the red pepper jalapeño vinegar and the smoky tomato sauce made with tomatoes we smoke on mesquite and apple wood. Both dips have a genuine Tex-Mex appeal, and they work well with the East Coast calamari (ours are from Point Judith, Rhode Island). The vinegar recipe was influenced by Robin Leach of *Lifestyles of the Rich and Famous* when we were in my kitchen at the Tatou Supper Club in New York, cooking with celebrities. He drizzled vinegar over dried smelts, which gave me the idea to add some spice to it and use sushi vinegar instead. We've been using it ever since at the restaurants. These dips also work with other fish and chicken. You don't need a deep fryer for this small amount of calamari. Any deep sauté pan will do. The secret to tenderness with calamari (in addition to quick cooking) is to soak them in milk before you cook them. The lactose in the milk helps make them tender.

Calamari

1½ pounds calamari, cleaned, cartilage removed, sliced into ¼-inch rings

1 cup (approximately) whole milk

1–2 cups all-purpose flour

½ teaspoon onion powder

½ teaspoon garlic powder

½ teaspoon dried basil

½ teaspoon dried oregano

½ teaspoon lemon powder (see Prep Tip)

Pinch of cayenne pepper

Pinch of kosher salt

1 teaspoon (approximately) black pepper

1–2 quarts canola or peanut oil for frying

Salt and white pepper to taste

Sauce

1 cup red pepper jalapeño vinegar (see recipe page 143)

1 cup smoky tomato sauce (see recipe page 136)

Prepare the calamari: Put the calamari in a bowl, cover with the milk, and refrigerate for 6 hours. In a separate large bowl, combine the flour, onion powder, garlic powder, basil, oregano, lemon powder, cayenne, and salt and black pepper. Put the flour mix in a gallon-size plastic food storage bag. Remove the calamari from the milk, drain, and shake off any excess milk.

Toss some of the calamari with the flour until the calamari is dry to the touch. Do this in several batches so you don't overcrowd the bag. Shake off excess coating and fry (also in several batches) in a deep-sided sauté pan (or deep fryer at 350 degrees) over high heat in canola or peanut oil until golden brown, 3 to 5 minutes. (Don't touch the pan for at least 30 seconds after putting in the calamari, then shake it gently to be sure the fish is not sticking to the pan.) Remove the calamari to a strainer and shake off excess fat. Immediately season with salt and white pepper.

To serve: Place the freshly cooked calamari in 4 individual bowls or 6-inch paella pans while still hot and serve the two sauces in separate ramekins or small bowls.

SERVES 4

PREP TIP: If you don't have lemon powder, dry out some lemon rind from one lemon for a day and powder it in a spice grinder.

FRIED OYSTERS SOUTHWEST

with Grilled Pineapple Serraño Salsa and
Roasted Red Pepper Saffron Rouille

I grew up in the East and still like Blue Point oysters from Long Island. However, when I came to Texas, I found some terrific things to serve with them. These oysters can be panfried or deep fried, but for such a small amount, a substantial sauté pan will do the trick. If you buy oysters already shucked, ask your fishmonger for the shells in which to serve them.

16 fresh oysters, preferably Blue Point
1 cup flour
1 egg, beaten
1 cup panko bread crumbs
1 quart canola or peanut oil
Pinch of kosher salt

1 sheet nonedible seaweed (optional)
  (see Shopping Tip)
1 cup roasted red pepper saffron rouille
  (see page 139)
1 cup grilled pineapple serraño salsa (see page 147)
Micro greens

Prepare the oysters: Shuck the oysters and clean the shells for later use. Place the flour, egg, and bread crumbs into 3 separate plates or wide soup bowls. Dip each oyster into the flour, then the egg, then the bread crumbs, and immediately flash fry it in a hot deep-sided sauté pan for 30 seconds on each side until golden brown. Don't crowd the pan, or they won't brown as well. Remove and immediately sprinkle some kosher salt over them.

To serve: Line each of 4 serving plates with the seaweed. Place 4 cleaned oyster shells on top of each dish. Spoon 1 teaspoon of the rouille inside the oyster shells. Place the oyster in the shell. Spoon 1 teaspoon of the salsa on top of the oyster. Garnish with micro greens.

SERVES 4

SHOPPING TIP: Ask your fishmonger for some seaweed for garnish. This is not the edible seaweed, but the kind that is used in tanks to keep live lobsters fresh. You can also use this type as a liner for fish you roast in the oven.

PREP TIP: The best visual on how to learn to shuck oysters is in Julia Child's book *The Way to Cook*. Always wear oyster shucking gloves for safety.

DEVILED TEXAS BLUE CRAB CAKE
with Roasted Corn Relish and Cilantro Ancho Chile Remoulade

Blue crabs are famous in the Chesapeake Bay, but they also thrive in the Gulf of Mexico. The term *blue crab* is also used for the canned lump crabmeat, some of which is really another species from Indonesia. Good lump crabmeat is available year-round in the refrigerator case of high-quality food stores. Never use the canned crabmeat that is sold next to tuna fish in the unrefrigerated sections. It is not the same thing. The secret of any good crab cake is not to manhandle it. Fold in the ingredients gently and as quickly as possible. The secret of these crab cakes is the meld of flavors from the smoky roasted corn relish and cilantro ancho chile remoulade and the sweet fish. Be sure to make a very fine dice of the onion, celery, and red pepper. This is known as *brunoise*.

Crab Cake

1 pound jumbo lump crabmeat

¼ cup very finely diced red onion

¼ cup very finely diced celery

¼ cup very finely diced red pepper

2 slices dried white bread, crusts removed
    and grated (with a box grater)

¼ cup skim milk

Salt and black pepper

1 lemon, juiced

Few drops of Tabasco to taste

1 teaspoon Old Bay Seasoning

1 teaspoon Worcestershire sauce

¼–½ cup fresh white bread or panko crumbs

2 tablespoons clarified (or whole) butter

Salad

2 cups field greens

½ cup (approximately) Italian dressing (store
    bought is fine)

1 cup roasted corn relish (see page 148)

½ cup cilantro ancho chile remoulade
    (see page 146)

Prepare the crabmeat: Combine the crabmeat, onion, celery, and red pepper; reserve. In a separate bowl, combine the dried bread and skim milk and let the bread absorb all the milk. This is called the *panada*. Gently mix the panada with the crab mixture and season with salt, pepper, lemon juice, Tabasco, Old Bay, and Worcestershire. Divide the crabmeat into 6 portions and shape each like an egg or round patty. Gently roll the crab cakes in bread crumbs and sauté in a little bit of clarified butter on medium heat until they are golden brown and the center is warm (155 degrees on an instant-read thermometer).

Prepare the salad: Toss the field greens with the Italian dressing and set aside.

To serve: Put some of the dressed salad greens on each plate and place 3 heaping tablespoons of the corn relish next to the greens. Drizzle the remoulade alongside the relish in a zigzag or other attractive pattern. Center the crab cake on the greens and relish.

SERVES 6

SHOPPING TIP: Field greens are any mixture of lettuce types, such as Lollo Rossa, green leaf, red leaf, oakleaf, mizuna, and tatsoi. Always gently wash and dry them before use.

PREP TIP: Clarified butter is the liquid part separated from the solids. Slowly melt butter in a saucepan until the solids sink to the bottom. Skim off any foam, then pour the golden liquid away from the solids. Clarified butter has a higher smoke point, so it is suitable for cooking over high heat.

AHI TUNA TARTARE
with Toasted White Sesame Seeds, Serraño, and Lemon Banyuls Vinaigrette

This delicious tartare came from internationally known chef Wayne Nish of New York's March restaurant during a sold out "Friends of Scott Cohen" wine and food event here in San Antonio. Wayne liked to use white soy sauce, but with his permission to play with it, I've made it more traditional. The magic here is how you cut the tuna. Rather than chop the fish or meat as you would with traditional tartare, make paper-thin slices quickly, as if you were slicing a celery stalk. You will need an extremely sharp sushi knife. This technique works well with other fish, such as salmon and flounder. Shaving rather than chopping preserves the oils in the fish, and thus the flavor. Do not add salt and pepper to this recipe because the soy is salty, and you want the other flavors to come through.

3 tablespoons white sesame seeds

Vinaigrette
2 tablespoons Banyuls vinegar (see Shopping Tips)
2 tablespoon light soy sauce
1 teaspoon lemon olive oil (or grate some lemon rind into olive oil)

Tuna Tartare
12 ounces raw sushi-grade ahi tuna, shaved
1 serraño chile pepper, seeded and minced

4 tablespoons chive oil (see recipe page 143)
Chopped chives

Prepare the seeds: Toast the sesame seeds on a sheet pan with low sides in a 350-degree oven for about 10 minutes until they are golden brown.

Prepare the vinaigrette: Combine the vinegar, soy sauce, and lemon olive oil in a blender or mini food processor.

Prepare the tartare: Shave the tuna and in a small bowl mix it with the serraño and vinaigrette.

To serve: Place a 3-inch ring mold in the center of a plate and fill it with about 3 ounces of the tuna tartare. Pack it down and remove the ring. Lightly top the tartare with the toasted sesame seeds and garnish the plate with chive oil and a few chopped chives. Serve cold.

SERVES 4

PREP TIP: You can use a tuna can as a ring mold or have a plumber cut some PVC pipe rings, which is what I use.

SHOPPING TIPS: Be sure to ask for sushi-grade tuna. The fish should have absolutely no odor, and the color should be bright red. Some less than scrupulous dealers dye their tuna to enhance the color.

Banyuls vinegar is made from the naturally sweet wine of a small seaside town in the Mediterranean called Banyuls-sur-Mer. It has an aroma of walnut, spice cake, vanilla, and licorice. If you absolutely cannot find this type, use a good balsamic vinegar.

HOT AND COLD SOUPS

Soup is a wonderful way to bring fabulous flavor to a simple form. The best part is that soups can often be made ahead, assembled, and brought to the perfect temperature just before serving. Chilled soup is gaining more credence as a first course, and some cooks use it as a dessert.

The biggest mistake cooks make with soup is overcooking. Make sure that the cooking time is just enough to heat the soup to where it is done or ready to be pureed, then pull it off the burner. The longer you cook your soup after that state, the more flavor is lost. Use the freshest products available for the season, and make sure vegetables are at their peak ripeness. For example, if you are making gazpacho, use tomatoes that are very ripe, or even a bit overripe.

Most of these recipes allow for generous portions, so you may have some leftovers.

CHILLED TEXAS MINT AND SUGAR SNAP PEA SOUP

BLACK BEAN SOUP
with Cilantro Yogurt

This hearty soup is one of my first creations as a chef, and it appeared in *Art Culinaire* magazine. It makes a great lunch, or even a dinner, with some melted cheese quesadillas, black bean salsa (see page 147), and a robust red wine. This soup is all about the beans, so buy the highest quality you can find from a reputable dealer. Examine the beans closely. They should have a nice black color and not appear to be "dusty." It really makes a difference. You'll need two bunches of cilantro: one for the soup and another for the yogurt cream, as well as garnish. Also, a day ahead, marinate in olive oil the vegetables, herbs, and bacon that go into the soup.

Beans

2 pounds dried black beans

Vegetables

1 red bell pepper, seeded and diced (save a small amount for garnish)

1 yellow bell pepper, seeded and diced (save a small amount for garnish)

1 poblano pepper, seeded and diced (save a small amount for garnish)

½ jalapeño, seeded and diced

1 red onion, peeled and diced

1 tablespoon cumin seeds

4 ounces diced bacon

1 cup olive oil

1 bunch cilantro, chopped

2 sprigs thyme, chopped

2 bay leaves

1 bulb garlic, peeled

Soup

2 quarts low-sodium chicken stock

2 tablespoons salt (approximately)

1 tablespoon black pepper

Cilantro Yogurt

1 cup nonfat plain yogurt

1 bunch cilantro, chopped (set aside a small amount of leaves for garnish)

Salt and black pepper

2 teaspoons diced tomato for garnish

2 teaspoons reserved diced peppers for garnish

1 avocado, quartered to make a fan (and dice a small amount)

Prepare the beans: A day ahead, put ¾ of the beans into a large pot. Put ¼ of the beans in a double piece of cheesecloth (sachet bag) so you can use them to make the salsa. (See recipe page 147.) Cover the beans, including those in the cheesecloth, in cold water and soak overnight.

Marinate the vegetables: Combine peppers, onion, cumin, bacon, oil, herbs, and garlic, and marinate in the refrigerator overnight.

Prepare the soup: The next day, sauté the marinated vegetables in a large soup pot until soft. Drain the black beans and add to the pot. Cover with chicken stock, bring to a boil, reduce heat, and simmer until beans are tender, about an hour. Season with salt and pepper and remove the gauze bag of beans for the salsa. When the soup cools, puree in a food processor, then strain it through a sieve.

Prepare cilantro yogurt: Combine yogurt, cilantro, and some salt and pepper in a small bowl.

To serve: Put soup into 4 bowls and make a zigzag pattern on top with the cilantro yogurt with a squeeze bottle or a spoon. Garnish with some of the salsa, diced tomato and peppers, and cilantro leaves. Make an avocado fan for each plate.

SERVES 4

SQUASH BLOSSOM ROASTED CORN HUITLACOCHE SOUP

This soup was inspired by the Mexican artist Frida Kahlo. When the movie *Frida* opened in 2002, we hosted a party at Las Canarias and created some recipes brought to us by the granddaughter of the artist Diego Rivera. Kahlo loved squash blossom soup, but the original was a no-frills recipe, which I thought would be even tastier with the addition of huitlacoche. Everybody fell in love with the soup, and it has been on our menu ever since. It's not only interesting and delicious, it's healthful. This soup is an outstanding appetizer before a meal, or as a meal in itself with a salad.

1 large yellow onion, finely chopped

4 tablespoons butter

2 ears of corn, kernels scraped off

3 poblano chiles, roasted, peeled, seeded, and cut in strips

1 cup coarsely chopped zucchini

4 garlic cloves, minced

8 ounces huitlacoche (see Shopping Tips)

2 cups sliced mushrooms (any kind)

4 cups squash blossoms, stems and pistils discarded, coarsely chopped (see Shopping Tips and Prep Tip)

6 cups low-fat and low-sodium chicken broth

Salt to taste

3 tortillas, cut in small squares (¼ x ¼ inch) and fried

½ cup (approximately) crème fraîche (can substitute sour cream)

1 small bunch cilantro

Prepare the soup: In a large saucepan over medium heat, sauté the onion in butter until translucent. Add the corn, chiles, zucchini, garlic, and huitlacoche and cook for 2 more minutes. Stir in the mushrooms and squash blossoms and cook for 4 minutes. Add the chicken broth, bring to a boil, and simmer for 10 to 12 minutes. Salt to taste.

To serve: Use wide soup bowls and garnish with tortilla squares, crème fraîche, and cilantro leaves.

SERVES 8 AS AN APPETIZER OR 4 AS A LIGHT MEAL

SHOPPING TIPS: The smoky, sweet flavor of this soup comes from the huitlacoche, a corn fungus that is also known as corn truffle and Mexican truffle. It would be difficult to get the native corn that is grown to create this delicacy, so we use the canned huitlacoche found in specialty and Mexican stores.

Squash blossoms from either winter or summer squash are yellow to orange in color and available from spring to fall in specialty produce markets. Sometimes you can find them in Latin, Italian, or Filipino stores. Choose blossoms with closed buds.

PREP TIP: Squash blossoms are extremely perishable, so don't keep them more than a day in the fridge. (You can freeze them in plastic bags, however.) Rinse them gently before you cut them, and use a sharp knife so as not to tear the delicate flesh.

ROASTED ASPARAGUS AND CURRIED APPLE SOUP
with Pecans

Pecans (pee-KAHNS as we say here) grow all over the place. The first time I went out to play golf when I got to San Antonio, I was taken to a course called Pecan Valley, about 15 miles away. The course was full of pecan trees, and you could shake the nuts right out of the branches. I thought Texas pecans would be perfect for an asparagus soup. In fact, they were more than perfect; they were awesome. I don't actually get the pecans from the golf course, but from Hill Country farms.

2 bunches asparagus, cut into 1-inch pieces

4 tablespoons olive oil

Salt and white pepper to taste

¼ pound diced cold butter

1 white onion, diced

3 stalks celery, diced

1 carrot, peeled and diced

1 tablespoon curry powder

2 Granny Smith apples, peeled and diced
   (save some for garnish)

¼ cup all-purpose flour

1 quart chicken broth

2 cups heavy cream

1 cup Texas pecans, toasted (see Prep Tip)

Toss the asparagus with the olive oil and season with the salt and white pepper. Put the asparagus on a sheet pan and roast in a 350-degree oven for about 20 minutes.

In a large soup pot, sweat the onions, celery, and carrots in the butter. Add the roasted asparagus and curry powder, then the apples, and stir until the edges of the apples begin to round off. Sprinkle in the flour and stir until it coats everything in the pot. Add the chicken broth and bring to a boil. Lower the heat and simmer for about 10 minutes. Add the cream and allow the soup to cook until all the vegetables are soft. With a hand blender (commonly called a stick mixer), blend the soup and season with more salt and white pepper. Strain the soup through a sieve and add the toasted pecans.

To serve: Garnish the soup bowls with some toasted pecans and diced apple, or even some reserved asparagus tips.

SERVES 8 AS AN APPETIZER OR 4 AS A LIGHT MEAL

PREP TIP: Toast the pecans on a sheet pan in a 350-degree oven for about 15 minutes. Remove from oven and set aside to cool.

CHILLED TEXAS MINT AND
SUGAR SNAP PEA SOUP

Mint grows profusely in the Texas sun, and it quenches the palate, which is good in a hot climate. I like the flavor that develops when it's paired with sugar snap peas, which taste like a cross between an asparagus and a snow pea. And like snow peas, sugar snap peas don't need to be shelled. Use them whole in the soup because they will be pureed. By the way, if this soup is not cooked enough, it will have a khaki green color instead of a nice bright green.

4 stalks celery, roughly chopped

1 white onion, roughly chopped

1½–2 pounds fresh sugar snap peas

2 quarts chicken broth

1 cup chopped fresh mint leaves

Salt and white pepper to taste

½ tomato, diced

1 ounce diced queso fresco cheese
    (see Shopping Tip)

Mint leaves

In a large pot, sweat the celery and onions. Add the peas and the chicken broth and bring to a boil. Lower heat to a simmer and continue to cook for about 15 minutes. Add half of the mint and continue to cook until all vegetables are soft. Remove the pot from the stove and place the soup in a metal container in an ice bath to chill rapidly. While the soup is cooling, add the rest of the mint and with a stick mixer, blend the soup until it is completely smooth. Season with salt and white pepper.

To serve: Garnish each bowl of soup with some diced tomato, cheese, and mint leaves.

SERVES 8 AS AN APPETIZER OR 4 AS A LIGHT MEAL

SHOPPING TIP: Queso fresco is a fresh cow's milk cheese, similar to farmer's cheese. It comes in tubs like cottage cheese and is found in Latin food stores.

BUTTERNUT SQUASH SOUP
with Pecans and Chervil

We have abundant summer and winter squash growing in the Hill Country, so it is a year-round treat. Butternut squash is a perfect canvas for allspice, cinnamon, cardamom, and maple syrup used to glaze the squash as it is roasting. This is an easy soup to make, and you can do it a day ahead and heat it up to serve. In an over-the-top presentation at the restaurants, we serve this with a wild rice fritter in the bottom of the soup bowl, and a garnish of shredded duck confit and cracklings, sautéed foie gras, toasted pecans, kernels of cooked wild rice, roasted corn, and a few sprigs of chervil. However, it is fine with the pecans and chervil, which tastes like a light version of Italian parsley, as garnish.

Glaze

3 ounces unsalted butter

3 tablespoons maple syrup

⅛ teaspoon ground allspice

⅛ teaspoon ground cinnamon

⅛ teaspoon ground cardamom

Pinch of ground nutmeg

Salt and black pepper to taste

Butternut Squash Soup

2 large butternut squash cut in half and seeded

2 ounces unsalted butter

½ yellow onion, diced

1 stalk celery, diced

1 carrot, peeled and diced

1 leek, white part only, diced

2 quarts chicken stock

20 pecans, toasted (see Prep Tip page 32)

4 sprigs fresh chervil

Prepare the glaze: In a small mixing bowl, combine the melted butter, maple syrup, allspice, cinnamon, cardamom, nutmeg, salt, and pepper to make a glaze.

Prepare the squash: Set the squash halves on an oiled sheet pan, cut side down, and roast for 20 to 25 minutes in a 400-degree oven. Turn over the squash and brush with the glaze. Continue roasting, brushing frequently with the glaze, until the squash is tender and golden brown, about 30 more minutes. (If it starts to darken, cover it with tinfoil.) Remove from oven and cool before scooping out the flesh with a large spoon.

Prepare the soup: In a large soup pot, heat the remaining butter and sauté the onion, celery, carrot, and leek until all ingredients are tender. Add the squash and season with salt and pepper. Add the chicken stock, bring just to a boil, and lower the heat to simmer until all of the vegetables are soft, about 35 minutes. Pour the soup into a food processor and puree. Adjust seasoning.

To serve: Pour soup into four separate wide bowls and garnish each dish with 4 or 5 pecans and a sprig of chervil.

SERVES 4

TORTILLA SOUP

Remember the movie *Tortilla Soup,* about the chef who lost his sense of taste but kept on cooking for his three daughters? Needless to say, it prompted a surge of interest in this traditional Mexican soup, which is a very big part of the culture of Texas. It's an easy soup to make, and you can serve it warm or chilled. If you have leftover cooked chicken, this is a good way to use it. Always buy fresh handmade tortillas. I like corn tortillas better than flour, but it's only a personal bias. Both types are good so long as they are fresh.

Chicken

1 boneless, skinless chicken breast

Salt and pepper for seasoning

1 to 2 tablespoons olive oil

Onion Puree

1 yellow onion, peeled and rough chopped

Soup

½ cup olive oil

1 onion, peeled and diced

1 jalapeño, seeded and diced

½ ancho chile, seeded and diced

5 cloves garlic, rough chopped

1 teaspoon cumin seeds, toasted in a dry sauté pan

2 sprigs epazote (see Shopping Tip)

4 corn tortillas, diced

8 very ripe tomatoes, diced

2 quarts chicken stock

2 tablespoons salt

1 tablespoon black pepper

2 corn tortillas, julienned

1 avocado, diced

1 red tomato, finely diced

1 yellow tomato, finely diced

¼ cup grated Monterey Jack cheese

Few sprigs of fresh epazote or cilantro

Prepare the chicken: Season the chicken breast with salt and pepper and pound it between two sheets of waxed paper or plastic wrap until thin. Sauté in 1 to 2 teaspoons of the olive oil until cooked through. When cooled, slice the chicken breast into thin julienned strips and set aside.

Prepare the onion puree: Puree the onion in the food processor and set aside.

Prepare the soup: Heat ½ cup of olive oil in a large saucepan. Add the diced onion and sauté until soft. Add the jalapeño, ancho, garlic, cumin seeds, epazote, and diced tortillas and sauté for another 2 minutes. Add the tomatoes, pureed onion, chicken stock, salt, and pepper, and bring to a boil. Reduce the heat and simmer until the vegetables are cooked tender, about 45 minutes. Strain through a sieve or chinois and reserve.

To serve: Arrange the chicken, tortillas, avocado, tomatoes, and Monterey Jack cheese in 4 wide soup plates. Ladle the soup over these and garnish with fresh epazote or cilantro leaves.

SERVES 4

SHOPPING TIP: Epazote is also called Mexican tea and is often served that way. Its flavor is a bit like cilantro. It is sold dry in Mexican stores. When you find it fresh, it's usually from somebody's garden.

CHILLED GAZPACHO
with Texas Blue Crab

As soon as the tomatoes are up in June, I drive over to Oak Hill Farms and see what I can get for that month's tasting menu. The soft-skinned plump tomatoes, right off the vine, inspired this summer soup. I lightened up the French and Spanish versions, which usually include bread crumbs to make it thick. It's important to marinate it for 24 hours, then put it into the food processor and blend to the consistency of tomato juice. Add tequila for an added kick and serve in tall glasses. Our guests beg me for the recipe.

3 unpeeled English cucumbers, rough chopped (see Shopping Tip)

1 red bell pepper, seeded, rough chopped

1 yellow bell pepper, seeded, rough chopped

1 green bell pepper, seeded, rough chopped

1 medium-size red onion, peeled, rough chopped

2 jalapeño peppers, rough chopped

4 garlic cloves, chopped

8–10 red beefsteak tomatoes, rough chopped

1 bunch cilantro, rough chopped (save some leaves for garnish)

1 bunch basil, rough chopped

½ bunch Mexican oregano (save some leaves for garnish)

½ cup olive oil

½ cup sherry vinegar (see Taste Tip)

6 tablespoons (about 2 shots) Patron tequila (or any good brand) (optional)

1 lime, juiced

Salt and black pepper to taste

Tomato juice for thinning the soup if necessary

½ pound Texas Gulf or other lump crabmeat, broken into small bits

Few sprigs fresh cilantro and Mexican oregano (optional)

Diced red, yellow, and green peppers for garnish

Prepare the soup: Marinate all ingredients except tomato juice, crabmeat, and garnish in a nonreactive bowl for 24 hours. Then put the mixture into a food processor set for a fine grind. If necessary, use tomato juice to adjust consistency. You want a medium-thick soup.

To serve: Fill tall glasses (or a white bowl) with the gazpacho and garnish with bits of crab, diced peppers, cilantro leaves, and Mexican oregano.

SERVES 8 TO 10

SHOPPING TIP: English cucumbers are long and thin. They are usually wrapped in plastic to retain the moisture, so they are not waxed like the more common varieties. Because they have very small seeds, they are sweeter than the others. They are available in upscale produce markets year-round.

TASTE TIP: Sherry vinegar has a sweet and nutty flavor that enhances the soup, so don't use a substitute here.

THE FRESHEST SALADS

and a Few Sandwiches

Salads are appetizers, side dishes, or meals in themselves. They can sometimes follow a meal, as they often do in Europe. A salad of fresh-picked greens is one of the most sublime culinary treats. At the restaurants we are fortunate to have all kinds of greens from Bluebonnet Farms. Some of the baby greens come to us still rooted in their planting medium, so they are literally picked just before they go into a salad.

Salads are colorful, fresh, and a natural backdrop to a flavorful dressing. And here is where many mistakes begin. Never overdress a salad. Dressing is meant to flavor the greens, not drown them. It is impossible to make the precise amount of dressing for any particular salad, especially small amounts, so store the leftover dressing for further use. The dressing recipes here usually provide much more than you need, so don't be tempted to use it all at once.

Always wash all greens carefully, and make sure they are dry before you dress them. You can prepare greens and dressing ahead of time and keep them in the fridge until just before serving, but don't dress the greens until just before serving so they appear on the table at their freshest and most beautiful.

MESCLUN, FENNEL, AND CANDIED PECAN SALAD

MESCLUN, FENNEL, AND CANDIED PECAN SALAD

with Lemon Basil Dressing

Fennel used to grow wild in this country, but Americans have never appreciated it as much as Europeans, who grow a smaller and more delicate variety used throughout the Mediterranean region. (The Italians call it *finócchio*.) With its licorice-like flavor, fennel is a great match with pecans, which are native to Texas and Georgia. Roast the pecans and make the dressing first, then toss the pecans into the salad just before serving. Mesclun is simply a name for young salad greens and can include arugula, dandelion greens, frisée, mizuna, oakleaf lettuce, radicchio, and sorrel. This salad calls for aged goat cheese (minimum of one year), a semihard cheese that can be shaved.

Pecans

1 tablespoon sugar

1 cup chopped pecans

Pinch of cayenne pepper

1 teaspoon water

Lemon Basil Dressing

1 bunch fresh lemon basil

1 shallot, coarsely chopped

6 tablespoons Champagne vinegar

2 tablespoons fresh lemon juice

2 eggs

¾ cup canola or safflower oil

¼ cup extra virgin olive oil

Salt and black pepper

Salad

1 medium-size fennel bulb

¼ pound firm, aged Texas goat cheese or
    Parmigiano-Reggiano

4 cups mesclun (as small and young as possible)

16 cherry or pear tomatoes, halved

Lemon basil dressing (from above)

Salt and freshly ground pepper

Toast the pecans: Preheat oven to 350 degrees. Toss sugar, pecans, and cayenne with teaspoon of water. Spread on an ungreased sheet pan and toast for 20 minutes; set aside.

Prepare the dressing: In a food processor, puree the lemon basil, shallot, Champagne vinegar, lemon juice, and eggs. Slowly add oils and process until it forms an emulsion. Dressing should be thin enough to lightly coat the salad greens. If it is too thick, thin it with cool water. Season with salt and pepper.

Prepare the salad: Shave fennel paper thin (use a mandoline for best results) and keep in ice water until ready to use. Drain and pat dry with a clean towel. Shave cheese paper thin. Toss mesclun, candied pecans, and tomatoes with ¼ to ½ cup dressing to lightly coat. Adjust seasoning.

To serve: Divide greens evenly among 4 or 8 plates and top with fennel and cheese. This also looks terrific in a margarita glass.

SERVES 4 (OR 8 AS AN APPETIZER)

PREP TIPS: Clean the mesclun gently by rinsing it and patting it dry between two towels. If you put it in a salad spinner, you will tear some of the delicate leaves. A salad with baby greens should be eaten within 10 minutes.

Gently squeeze some of the tomatoes after they are halved so you get rid of excess juice that will dilute the dressing.

BABY ICEBERG LETTUCE SALAD
with Goat Cheese, Toasted Almonds, Sun-dried Cranberries,
Pickled Red Onions, and Creamy Apple Cider Vinaigrette

A young soft goat cheese is required for this recipe. We use Texas Bluebonnet hydro greens produced by my friend Emile, who used to be a cattle farmer. These lettuce heads are very tight and a little smaller than a grapefruit. Emile delivers these greens alive to me, so they are fresh until the moment they are on the diner's plate. One head serves two people. You can substitute baby Boston lettuce if you can't find the iceberg.

Almonds

¼ cup sliced almonds

Apple Cider Vinaigrette

1 teaspoon minced shallots

½ Granny Smith apple, peeled, cored, and minced

1 teaspoon Dijon mustard

2 teaspoons honey

⅛ cup apple cider vinegar

⅛ cup safflower or other light vegetable oil

Salt and white pepper to taste

Salad

2 heads baby iceberg, cut into quarters

½ cup fresh goat cheese (less than 12 months old)

4 tablespoons sun-dried cranberries

4 tablespoons pickled red onions (see recipe
    page 148)

Toast the almonds: Spread almonds on a sheet pan and place in preheated 350-degree oven for 3 to 5 minutes until just browned.

Prepare the dressing: In a blender, puree the shallots, apples, mustard, honey, and apple cider vinegar. While the blender is running slowly, add in oil to form an emulsion. Season with salt and white pepper and set aside.

Assemble the salad: Place two quarters of a lettuce head on each plate, leaning them against each other with the sharp ends up. Drizzle ⅛ to ¼ cup of dressing on the lettuce and around the plate. Sprinkle 3 or 4 pieces of goat cheese, some dried cranberries, and toasted almonds around the plate and on the salad. Top the salad with the pickled onions, about 1 tablespoon per portion.

SERVES 4

PREP TIP: To clean baby lettuce heads, fill a bowl with ice cold water and put the heads in the water for 2 minutes, moving them around. Lift out of the water and drain on paper towels.

LAVENDER FIELDS AT BECKER VINEYARDS

CRISPY HEARTS OF ROMAINE
with Tortilla Croutons and Ancho Caesar Dressing

This is the signature salad at Las Canarias. With its fresh produce and smoky flavor, it represents what the Texas Hill Country is all about. I have never been able to take it off the menu. Make the dressing and croutons first, and put the salad together just before serving. Buy fresh tortillas when you can, and avoid machine-made tortillas, identified by their uniform shape.

Tortilla Croutons
1 tablespoon olive oil
1 teaspoon red chile flakes
1 teaspoon chopped fresh rosemary
¼ teaspoon black pepper
¼ teaspoon salt or to taste
2 6-inch fresh flour tortillas, cut into ½-inch
    squares

Ancho Caesar Dressing
1 ancho chile pepper
1 tablespoon minced fresh cilantro
1 teaspoon minced garlic
2 teaspoons minced shallots
1 anchovy, minced

½ tablespoon Dijon mustard
1 egg
½ cup red wine vinegar
1 teaspoon Worcestershire sauce
½ teaspoon Tabasco sauce
1 cup canola oil
¼ cup olive oil
1 teaspoon coarsely ground black pepper
Salt and freshly ground pepper

Salad
2 heads romaine hearts, bottom root removed
¼ cup Parmesan, grated or shredded on a box
    grater
Tortilla croutons (from above)
1 medium-size tomato, diced small

Prepare the croutons: Preheat oven to 275 degrees. In a large bowl, combine olive oil, chile flakes, rosemary, and black pepper. Toss in the tortilla squares and transfer to a sheet pan and bake for 10 minutes or until the tortilla squares turn golden brown and dry out. Season with salt and pepper.

Prepare the dressing: Steep the ancho pepper in hot water for about 30 minutes to reconstitute it. Puree the pepper in a blender and add cilantro, garlic, shallots, anchovy, mustard, egg, vinegar, and Worcestershire and Tabasco sauces. Slowly drizzle in the oils, allowing the blender to run the entire time and until an emulsion forms. Add a bit more vinegar or some water if the dressing is too thick. Season with salt and pepper and refrigerate.

Assemble the salad: Toss lettuce and dressing together and arrange on a 10-inch salad plate. Top the salad with the Parmesan cheese, croutons, and diced tomato.

SERVES 4

PREP TIPS: Use romaine hearts and not the whole head to get a better salad without losing a lot of leaves.

When you grate or shred cheese with a box grater, try using different holes for a more interesting look for the cheese.

ORGANIC FIELD GREENS
with Pear Tomatoes, Garlic Nut Crunch, Smoked Bacon, Crumbled Blue Cheese, and Lemon Basil Dressing

Organic field greens have a stronger and fresher taste, so whenever possible I like to use them. Lemon basil, sweeter than other basils, is the most popular variety in Texas and practically grows wild. It is a fine complement to smoked bacon and blue cheese, and a natural with tomatoes. Bacon really makes this salad, so be adventurous and try new quality types, such as Maverick from Colorado. Or go on the Internet and join a bacon club. A garlic nut crunch (granola and oil) adds another texture.

Garlic Nut Crunch

½ cup granola

1 tablespoon garlic oil (or mince a garlic clove in some olive oil)

Lemon Basil Dressing

½ cup chopped fresh lemon basil

½ tablespoon minced shallots

½ cup Champagne wine vinegar

1 lemon, juiced

2 whole eggs

½ cup olive oil

1 cup canola oil

Salt and pepper

Salad

4 cups assorted organic field greens

½ cup crumbled blue cheese

4 slices high-quality smoked bacon, cooked and chopped

½ cup garlic nut crunch (from above)

12 pear tomatoes cut in half

½ small red onion, shaved into very fine slivers with a mandoline

Prepare the nut crunch: Moisten the granola with garlic oil and toast on a sheet pan for 10 minutes in a 350-degree oven.

Prepare the dressing: In a blender, puree the lemon basil, shallots, vinegar, lemon juice, and eggs. Slowly drizzle in both oils while the blender is running to form an emulsion. Add salt and pepper to taste.

Prepare the salad: In a large bowl, toss field greens, blue cheese, bacon bits, and garlic nut crunch with lemon basil dressing to coat lightly.

To serve: Arrange 6 tomato halves around the side of each 8-inch plate and put a mound of salad in the center. Top with the shaved red onions. Serve this right away.

SERVES 4

YOUNG SPINACH AND GOAT CHEESE SALAD
with Pecans, Sun-dried Tomatoes, and Grilled Onion Vinaigrette

The cheese and sun-dried tomatoes give this salad a delicious earthy flavor. We use Texas Yellow Bell or Fredericksburg goat cheese, which has a soft consistency. For a different dynamic, try it with a semihard cheese, such as smoked Gouda or smoked cheddar. We serve a cheese tray at Las Canarias with the best of local and international cheeses. Our waiters describe each cheese to our guests, so they get a chance to try something new.

½ large red onion

Grilled Onion Vinaigrette
1 tablespoon Dijon mustard
1 teaspoon minced garlic
½ cup red wine vinegar
½ cup olive oil
1 cup canola oil
Salt and white pepper

Salad
4 cups cleaned baby spinach
½ cup fresh goat cheese (and a bit more for
    garnish)
½ cup toasted pecans (and a few more for garnish)
    (see Prep Tip page 32)
½ cup sun-dried tomatoes steeped in olive oil, cut
    into quarters

Prepare the onion: Slice the onion and grill slices until soft.

Prepare the dressing: In a blender, puree grilled onions, mustard, garlic, and red wine vinegar. Slowly drizzle in the oils to form an emulsion and season with salt and white pepper.

Prepare the salad: Toss spinach with goat cheese, pecans, tomatoes, and dressing.

To serve: Use a 3- or 4-inch ring mold to shape the salad in the center of a wide white plate. The oil from the sun-dried tomatoes will bleed onto the plate, adding a golden outline. Garnish with the extra pecans and goat cheese.

SERVES 4

PREP TIP: The grilled onions make the dressing most distinctive. You can grill them on a stove-top grill, but if you happen to have a barbecue grill, that will make them taste even better. They pick up the lingering smoke flavors, especially if you use wood.

HEARTS OF PALM AND BIBB LETTUCE
with Mozzarella, Beefsteak Tomatoes, and Balsamic Vinaigrette

We have our own mozzarella maker in Dallas. Paula Lambert fell in love with this fresh cheese when she visited Italy many years ago, and because she could not find a real mozzarella cheese here, she decided to make it herself. Made daily in Dallas, Lambert's fresh cheese is in high demand. The mild but earthy flavors of the cheese and hearts of palm are the perfect backdrop for the sweet tang of the balsamic vinaigrette. Bibb and Boston are names for butterhead lettuce. A Kentucky farmer named Bibb developed the variety, also known as limestone lettuce because of the soil in that state that also grows terrific thoroughbred horses.

Balsamic Vinaigrette

1 cup balsamic vinegar

1 shallot, minced

1 clove garlic, minced

2 egg yolks

2 teaspoons Dijon mustard

1½ cups canola or safflower oil

½ cup olive oil

Salt and pepper

3 tablespoons chopped fresh tarragon

Salad

1 (14- or 16-ounce) can hearts of palm, cut into ½-inch rounds

1 cup fresh Dallas or other mozzarella, diced into ½-inch cubes

1 large beefsteak tomato, diced into ½-inch cubes

Creamy balsamic vinaigrette (from above)

4 heads baby Boston or Bibb lettuce

1 bunch scallions, sliced into ⅛-inch slivers (use entire scallion)

4 tablespoons fresh opal basil, cut into thin strips (chiffonade) (see Shopping Tip)

Prepare the dressing: In a blender, mix the balsamic vinegar, shallot, garlic, egg yolks, and mustard. Add the oils while the blender is running to form an emulsion. Season with salt and pepper. Mix in the tarragon after the blender is turned off, and reserve dressing in the refrigerator.

Prepare the salad: In a large bowl, combine the hearts of palm, mozzarella, diced tomatoes, and enough of the dressing to coat everything.

To serve: Place the salad in the center of a round plate and set the head of baby lettuce on top. Drizzle some of the dressing on top of and around the lettuce. Garnish the plate with the scallions and basil chiffonade.

SERVES 4

PREP TIP: If you can get fresh hearts of palm, blanch them in boiling water with a squeeze of lemon about 3 to 5 minutes, then shock them in ice water. Hearts of palm grow in South America, Hawaii, and some parts of southern Florida.

SHOPPING TIP: Most basil is green, but opal is purple and spikes up the color palette for this dish. Look for evenly colored leaves. Store the leftover basil wrapped in a damp paper towel and refrigerate in a plastic bag.

GRIDDLED HAM AND CHEESE FOCACCIA SANDWICH WITH MIXED GREENS

This is the best ham and cheese sandwich you will ever eat. The ham is oven baked, the cheese is English cheddar, the tomatoes are juicy-ripe red beefsteak, and the bread is sun-dried tomato focaccia. Shaved Granny Smith apple adds a bit of tartness, and the endive and other greens round it out. It's important to use a high-quality baked sliced ham such as Boar's Head or Hormel, or it won't stand up to the cheese. Use a good English cheddar like Keene's or something comparably sharp from Vermont. You will put this sandwich into the oven three times as you layer the ingredients. But you'll see, it will be worth it.

Salad

½ Granny Smith apple, shaved thin and sliced into
    1-inch strips

2 endive, julienned

2 cups mixed greens or mesclun

4 tablespoons buttermilk dressing (see page 145)

Sandwich

4 sun-dried tomato focaccia, about 3 by 4 inches,
    each cut in half*

1 pound baked ham, sliced thin

1 ripe beefsteak tomato, sliced ¼-inch thick

8 slices English cheddar, about ¼-inch thick
    (about 3×4 inches overall to fit bread slices)

For the salad: In a small bowl, toss the apple, endive, and greens with the buttermilk dressing and set aside.

For the sandwich: Toast the focaccia in a tabletop toaster oven or under the broiler. Place the ham on top of 4 pieces of the toast and warm it up in the oven, being sure to cover all the bread so it doesn't burn. When the ham is heated, put the tomato on top and return to the oven to heat it about 2 minutes. Then top it with the cheese and return to the oven until it is melted.

To serve: Top each sandwich with the salad and remaining slice of bread. Cut into three equal pieces and serve. This sandwich pairs well with a simple potato salad or celeriac remoulade.

★You can substitute regular focaccia and spread it with some chopped sun-dried tomatoes.

SERVES 4

OPEN-FACED SWEET SHRIMP SALAD SANDWICH

Who doesn't love shrimp salad? When the shrimp is fresh from the Gulf of Mexico, its sweetness lends itself to a salad spiked with some Mexican lime, which is similar to key lime, but more acidic, flavorful, and juicy.

Shrimp

1 pound sweet small shrimp (21–25 count)

Salad

2 tablespoons mayonnaise

1 teaspoon Dijon mustard

1 tablespoon minced red onion

1 tablespoon minced celery

½ teaspoon ground coriander seed

1 teaspoon chopped fresh dill

Pinch of cayenne pepper

½ Mexican lime, juiced

Salt and white pepper

Sandwich

4 slices focaccia bread, 3×3 inches square,
        cut in half to form triangles

24 thin slices of cucumber

12 thin slices of avocado

4 sprigs fresh dill

Prepare the shrimp: Clean and devein the shrimp, and cook in boiling water for a few minutes until they turn pink. Drain and put the shrimp into a metal bowl, then place the bowl into an ice bath to stop the cooking. Be sure to chill the cooked shrimp thoroughly before making the salad. Cut into small dice, about ¼×¼ inch.

Prepare the salad: In a large bowl, combine the shrimp with the mayonnaise, mustard, red onion, celery, coriander, dill, cayenne, lime juice, salt, and white pepper. Refrigerate until ready to use.

Prepare the sandwiches: Toast the bread in a toaster or under the broiler. Place two triangle-shaped halves next to each other, longest sides together, on a round plate. Line each slice of bread first with cucumber slices, then top them with avocado slices. Using a ring mold, put ½ cup of the shrimp salad on top of the avocado on each plate (the salad will straddle both pieces of bread). Garnish with a dill sprig and serve chilled.

SERVES 4

LOBSTER CLUB SANDWICH ON BRIOCHE
with Apples, Tomatoes, Avocado, Smoked Bacon, and Herbed Mayonnaise

Lobsters don't readily grow in Texas, but they sure taste good with the apples, tomatoes, and other foods that do grow here. This rich sandwich is made with Love Creek apples, romaine, red beefsteak tomatoes, avocados from Mexico, hickory smoked bacon, and herbed mayonnaise. Buy fresh lobster from a fishmonger who will cook it for you. This is a tasty treat for a weekend picnic served with chilled Chablis.

Herbed Mayonnaise

¼ teaspoon chopped fresh parsley

¼ teaspoon chopped fresh thyme

¼ teaspoon chopped fresh oregano

1 lemon, juiced

2 cups mayonnaise (homemade aioli or Hellman's)

Sandwich

12 very thin brioche slices, toasted (or Pepperidge Farm thin-sliced white)

2 tablespoons herbed mayonnaise (from above)

8 romaine lettuce leaves

4 beefsteak tomatoes, sliced

4 slices bacon, cooked

4 ounces cooked lobster, sliced paper thin

1 Love Creek or Granny Smith apple, sliced paper thin

1 avocado, sliced

12 Pesca or other gourmet potato chips, such as Kettle or Miss Vicky's

4 sweet piquant peppers (see Flavor Tip)

Prepare the dressing: Mix the herbs and lemon juice with mayonnaise and set aside.

For the sandwich: Each sandwich requires three slices of toasted bread. Spread each slice with the mayonnaise. Layer the lettuce, tomatoes, and bacon on one slice of bread, cover with the second slice. Layer that slice with lobster, apples, avocado, and cover. Use toothpicks to hold the sandwich together. Cut it in half on the bias and serve with the chips and peppers.

SERVES 4

FLAVOR TIP: Piquant are African cherry peppers about the same size as cherry tomatoes. They have good heat without being too hot or too mild.

THE FUN OF FISH

Fish is fun to cook and eat. Many chefs love to cook fish because they can do so much more with it than they can with a piece of meat. It is also a clean, fresh flavor when prepared just right, which means cooking the freshest fish in the simplest way. Fish has become an extremely important part of a healthy diet. Today, we get fresh fish from all over the world with fast delivery services. That means fish can be out of the water for a day or two. Ten years ago fish could be out of the water for a week, which explains why so few Americans ate fish. *Pesca* means "fishing" in Spanish, and at Pesca on the River, we feature the freshest seafood flown in daily from around the world, with a focus on wild fish.

CRISPY SKIN RED SNAPPER CIOPPINO

HERBED RED SNAPPER
with Sun-dried Tomatoes and Pine Nuts

The spicy bean paste adds a pleasant zing to this otherwise Mediterranean dish with its lemon, garlic, tomatoes, and parsley.

4 (7-ounce) red snapper fillets with skin on

4 teaspoons Chinese hot bean paste

5 tablespoons chopped fresh flat-leaf parsley
(and a bit more for garnish)

1 tablespoon chopped chives (and a bit more
for garnish)

2 tablespoons all-purpose flour

1 garlic clove, minced

1 teaspoon pine nuts, toasted

12 sun-dried tomatoes, whole or
cut in half lengthwise

½ lemon, juiced

¼ cup olive oil

Salt and black pepper

Approximately 4 teaspoons olive oil for frying

With a sharp knife, score the skin of the snapper (see Prep Tips). Spread the bean paste on the skin evenly, using about 1 teaspoon for each fillet. Mix the chopped parsley and chives together and sprinkle over the skin, patting it down with a piece of waxed paper. Lightly dust each fillet with flour. Sauté the fillets skin side down in an oiled hot cast iron or nonstick sauté pan until golden brown, about 3 to 4 minutes per side, just until the flesh flakes when you touch it with a fork. Remove and set aside. Deglaze the pan with 1 teaspoon of olive oil. Add minced garlic, toasted pine nuts, sun–dried tomatoes, lemon juice, and ¼ cup olive oil. Season with salt and pepper.

To serve: Place fish in the middle of a dinner plate and drizzle the sauce lightly around the fish, touching the edges of the dish. Sprinkle on some of the chopped parsley and chives.

SERVES 4

PREP TIPS: Scoring the skin of meat or fish, say, in a diamond pattern, is not only decorative, it is a way to let flavors mingle and absorb into the flesh. It also allows excess fat to drain off. Use a sharp knife and make a crosshatch design.

When you need to sauté fish on extremely high heat, use an 8- or 9-inch cast iron or nonstick pan for best results. This allows you to maintain high heat with less risk of burning the food.

ROASTED CHILEAN SEA BASS
with Baby Bok Choy–Asian Slaw

Chilean sea bass is a marketing name for the tooth fish, which is not a very glamorous moniker. You can also use halibut for this dish. Prepare the slaw first. Slice all the vegetables so they are approximately the same size. You want to do the bok choy in a lengthwise chiffonade. Although it's easy to cut carrots into matchsticks, the onion, fennel, and jicama take a bit more effort. Cut the onion in half lengthwise, then make thin slices from each half. The same goes for the fennel bulb and jicama.

Slaw

2 heads baby bok choy
½ small red onion
1 carrot, peeled
½ medium-size fennel bulb
½ medium-size jicama
1 teaspoon whole mustard seeds
2 tablespoons sushi vinegar
1 tablespoon sugar
5–6 threads fresh saffron (see Prep Tip)
¼ cup olive oil
Salt and white pepper to taste

Fish

1½ pounds sea bass cut into 4 fillets of
    about 6 ounces each
Salt and black pepper for seasoning
1 tablespoon olive oil

1 English cucumber, peeled and sliced paper
    thin lengthwise
4 tablespoons chile-spiked oil (see page 143)
Micro greens

For the slaw: Slice all the vegetables as described in above headnote. In a large bowl, toss together the bok choy, onion, carrot, fennel, and jicama, and set aside. Preheat a medium-size saucepan over medium heat and add the mustard seeds. As soon as the seeds begin to pop, in about 1 minute, add the vinegar, sugar, and saffron. Bring the mixture to a boil, lower the heat, and simmer for about 3 minutes to extract all of the color from the saffron. Remove pot from the heat and immediately pour most of the mixture over the vegetable slaw, saving about ¼ cup for garnish. Add the olive oil and toss. Season with salt and white pepper and allow the slaw to marinate for at least 30 minutes. (It will stay fresh for up to 24 hours in the refrigerator.)

For the fish: Preheat oven to 350 degrees. Season the fillets with the salt and black pepper. In a hot sauté pan, pour just enough olive oil to cover the bottom of the pan (about 1 tablespoon). When the oil begins to roll on the pan (in a minute or two), gently place the fish in the pan. Don't move the fish for at least 30 seconds, so it will pick up a nice golden color. Then flip it over and put the pan into the oven for about 5 minutes or until the fish just begins to flake. Don't overcook, or the fish will dry out.

To serve: Place a mound of the slaw in the center of each wide soup bowl. Wrap a slice of the cucumber around the slaw to pull it together. (As long as the cucumber is moist and thin, it will hold.) Place the fish on top of the slaw, and drizzle the reserved vinaigrette into the bowl. Drizzle some of the chile-spiked olive oil on top of that, and garnish with micro greens.

SERVES 4

PREP TIP: Spanish saffron comes fresh and usually in a can or a small plastic bag. Once you open it, store the remaining saffron in a ziplock bag in a cool area, about 50 to 60 degrees.

SEARED DIVER SEA SCALLOPS

with Lemon Caper Couscous, Mesclun Greens, and
Texas Ruby Red Grapefruit—Port Sauce

The Ruby Red grapefruit spikes up the sweetness of the scallops, and the port reduction adds a richness to the dish that is unbeatable. Two cups of 10-year-old port seems a lot, but it reduces down to a delicious sauce. You'll need a total of about 8 or 9 fresh grapefruit for this dish—about 6 to squeeze for juice for the sauce and vinaigrette and more for segments for the salad. Always sear scallops quickly in a very hot pan so the inside remains soft.

Vinaigrette

1 Texas Ruby Red grapefruit
1 Mexican lime
1 Texas Valley (or similar) navel orange
3 tablespoons Champagne vinegar
2 ounces mosto olive oil (see Shopping Tip)
3 ounces safflower oil
Salt and white pepper

Couscous

1 cup Moroccan couscous
1 cup water
2 tablespoons capers
1 tablespoon herbes de Provence
1 lemon, zested and juiced
Salt and white pepper

Sauce

2 cups freshly squeezed Texas Ruby Red
    grapefruit juice
2 cups 10-year-old port wine
¼ pound (1 stick) cold unsalted butter

Salad

4 cups mesclun
1 grapefruit, segmented

Scallops

2 pounds U/10 diver scallops (up to 10 per pound)
Salt and black pepper
3 tablespoons olive oil

1 grapefruit, segmented
Candied grapefruit zest (optional, see page 151)

For the vinaigrette: Juice 1 grapefruit and the lime and orange. Whisk in vinegar, olive and saf-flower oils, salt and white pepper. Set aside.

For the couscous: Grate the lemon zest and set aside. In a medium-size saucepan, bring the water to a boil and add couscous, capers, herbes de Provence, grated lemon zest and juice, and salt and white pepper. Turn off heat and let stand covered for 20 minutes.

For the sauce: In a saucepan, reduce port and grapefruit juice down to a syrup. Whisk in cold butter slowly until the consistency of a slightly thin ketchup.

For the mesclun salad: Segment the remaining grapefruit and toss segments with mesclun and vinaigrette.

For the scallops: Season the scallops with salt and black pepper and sear in an oiled sauté pan on medium-high heat until caramelized. Flip over and sear for 5 seconds more. Remove from pan and reserve.

To serve: Pack about ½ cup couscous into a round mold and place it in center of each 10-inch round or 8-inch oval plate. Place mesclun salad at 12 o'clock position and place 5 seared scallops in a pyramid at 6 o'clock. Drizzle each dish with the port sauce, and garnish with grapefruit segments and candied grapefruit zest.

SERVES 4

SHOPPING TIP: Mosto oil is lemon-flavored olive oil. If you can't find it in your Italian or gourmet market, simply put some grated lemon peel into the olive oil.

SHRIMP SCAMPI LINGUINI
with Squash, Tomatoes, and Garlic Lemon Oil

This is my take on a classic, using fresh local vegetables—zucchini, yellow squash, and tomatoes. We give it a Mediterranean flavor with parsley, garlic, and lemon. First prepare the shrimp, then the vegetables and the crust, and cook the pasta at the end, just before serving. Everything is tossed together in a large sauté pan; then each individual ovenproof dish is coated with the parsley crust and put under a broiler for a few minutes.

Shrimp
12 shrimp, 16/20 size
Salt and black pepper for seasoning
2 tablespoons olive oil

Parsley Crust
4 tablespoons chopped fresh flat-leaf parsley
2 tablespoons chopped garlic
1 cup panko bread crumbs
4 teaspoons olive oil

Linguini
½ 8-ounce package linguini

Vegetables
1 zucchini, sliced into ¼-inch rounds
1 yellow squash, sliced into ¼-inch rounds
1 tomato, diced
2 tablespoons minced garlic
4 lemons, juiced

4 fried parsley sprigs (see recipe page 153)

For the shrimp: Clean, peel, and butterfly the shrimp. Season with salt and pepper, and sauté in oil in a hot pan until they turn pink. Set aside.

For the parsley crust: Combine parsley, garlic, and bread crumbs in a food processor and grind to a fine consistency. If necessary, add a bit of olive oil to avoid clumps. Set aside.

For the linguini: Boil linguini in a large pot of salted water until al dente. Drain and set aside, reserving some of the water.

For the vegetables: Sauté the squashes and tomatoes in olive oil with minced garlic until just tender. Add the linguini and lemon juice, and season with salt and pepper. If necessary, thin out with a bit of the reserved linguini water. Place in 4 large individual bowls and put the shrimp on top. Sprinkle with parsley crust, and put the bowls under the broiler until the crust browns, about 1 to 2 minutes.

To serve: Garnish with fried parsley.

SERVES 4

CRISPY SKIN RED SNAPPER CIOPPINO

Cioppino is a classic fish stew that began with Italian immigrants in San Francisco. Similar to bouillabaisse, it is often made with several fish. This version has a fragrant tomato-based broth over a bed of linguini and sea beans with a crispy red snapper fillet from the Gulf of Mexico. Sea beans are slightly salty. If they are hard to find, you can substitute haricots verts. The secret is to sear and then oven roast the snapper so that its crispy skin remains when you put the broth over it. The linguini can be made ahead and so can the Parmesan *tuile* garnish (see page 153). (You will end up with more broth than you need, so freeze the remainder and use it for any number of pasta dishes.) Serve this with crunchy bread and a robust red wine.

Pasta
½ pound fresh sweet squid ink linguini
   (see Shopping Tips)
Salt
Water for boiling

Fish
4 6-ounce red snapper fillets with the skin on
2 tablespoons all-purpose flour
4 tablespoons canola or olive oil

Sea Beans
2 cups sea beans (see Shopping Tips)

Chopped Tomatoes
2 fresh tomatoes, chopped
2 tablespoons olive oil
1 teaspoon minced garlic

Broth
¼ cup olive oil (not extra virgin)
2 tablespoons sliced garlic
1 large yellow onion, medium diced
1 bunch leeks, medium diced
1 teaspoon chopped fresh oregano
1 teaspoon chopped fresh rosemary
3 teaspoons chopped fresh thyme
1 teaspoon chopped fresh basil
Pinch of saffron (see Taste Tip)
1 tablespoon crushed red pepper
1 teaspoon toasted and ground coriander seed
2 tablespoons chopped fresh flat-leaf parsley
½ cup red wine vinegar
½ cup balsamic vinegar
4 ounces tomato puree
1 quart fish or chicken stock
2 cups clam juice
1 (28-ounce) can plum tomatoes
Salt and black pepper to taste

4 Parmesan *tuiles* (see recipe page 153)
Micro greens

Prepare the pasta: Cook linguini in large pot of salted water until al dente. Drain and rinse in cold water to stop the cooking; set aside.

Prepare the fish: Put 1 tablespoon of oil for each fillet in a skillet and turn to semihigh heat. Lightly dust the fish with flour and sear skin side down for 2 minutes. Turn over and sear again for another 2 minutes. Cook until medium or starting to flake. Remove from heat.

Prepare the sea beans: Blanch the sea beans in boiling salted water for 1 or 2 minutes. Drain and immediately put them into an ice bath to stop the cooking. Once cooled, drain and set aside.

Prepare the chopped tomatoes: Sauté the fresh tomatoes with the minced garlic in olive oil until just soft. Don't let the garlic brown, or it will become bitter. Set aside.

Prepare the broth: In a large pot, heat oil and add sliced garlic, onions, and leeks. Allow them to sweat until soft, but don't let them caramelize. Add oregano, rosemary, thyme, basil, saffron, red pepper, coriander, and parsley and continue cooking for 2 minutes. Add both vinegars and cook until reduced by a third. Add tomato puree, fish (or chicken) stock, clam juice, and plum tomatoes. Cook for 30 minutes and check consistency, which should be like a light broth. Add salt and pepper if needed. Add the sautéed chopped tomatoes at the end. Total cooking time is about 45 minutes.

To serve: Warm the pasta and sea beans by tossing with some of the hot broth. Place a bed of linguini and some sea beans in the bottom of each wide soup bowl, and put the red snapper on top of them. Ladle enough cioppino broth into each bowl to reach the fish, but do not submerge it. Garnish with a Parmesan *tuile* and micro greens.

SERVES 4

SHOPPING TIPS: Sea beans, also known as glasswort and marsh samphire, look like marsh grass and grow wild along seacoasts. They have spiky cactus-like leaves and a briny taste. They need to be blanched first to soften them.

Squid ink (black) linguini is available fresh in many gourmet stores. If you can't find it, you may substitute ½ pound of regular linguini.

PREP TIP: Be sure to submerge the chopped leeks in a bowl of cold water to remove any sand from between the layers. Take them out of the water and let drain before cooking.

TASTE TIP: Saffron is a critical ingredient to this recipe, and the best type is Spanish. The pistils are long and not chopped up. Saffron's expensive, but you only need a little bit, and it keeps in the fridge for a few months.

STEAK TUNA AU POIVRE
with Cognac Green Peppercorn Sauce

Steak au poivre, or pepper steak, is a fairly well-known dish, especially in France, where it originated. However, coating a thick tuna steak with cracked black pepper creates a wonderful flavor and texture that is lighter than beef, but with the same heft as beef. I created this dish for our sister restaurant, Pesca on the River, where we serve lighter fare. In Texas every menu must have steak, so here we have something just like steak but much lower in calories. The Cognac green peppercorn sauce adds the finishing touch. I like to serve this with grilled asparagus and haystack potatoes (see page 103).

Sauce

1 tablespoon minced garlic

1 tablespoon minced shallots

2 tablespoons vegetable oil

1 cup Cognac

2 cups heavy cream

1 bay leaf

2 cloves star anise

6 fresh whole green peppercorns

6 sprigs fresh thyme

1 cup veal stock (or ¼ cup demi-glace)

Salt and white pepper

Tuna

4 block-cut ahi (yellow fin) tuna steaks,
  about 7 ounces each (see Shopping Tip)

Butcher-cracked black pepper (see Prep Tips)

4 tablespoons grape seed oil

Micro greens

For the sauce: Sauté the garlic and shallots in a saucepan with 2 tablespoons oil over medium heat until they begin to sweat but not caramelize. Remove the pan from the stove and add the cognac to deglaze the pan; bring to a simmer and cook for 10 minutes. Add the heavy cream, bay leaf, anise, green peppercorns, and thyme and reduce by half, about 8 to 10 minutes, until the sauce just coats the back of a spoon. Add the veal stock and continue cooking until the sauce is a very light brown. Season with salt and white pepper. Set aside and keep warm.

For the tuna: Lightly crust the tuna with the cracked black pepper. Place the tuna in a smoking hot pan with the grape seed oil. Sear quickly on all sides until lightly browned; remove and allow to rest. Tuna should be served rare. A 7-ounce block-cut piece should take about 30 to 45 seconds in a very hot pan.

To serve: For each serving, cut a tuna steak in half and place the halves on the far ends of a plate. Place 5 grilled asparagus across the center of the plate and on the far right side of the plate, make a stack with haystack potatoes. Drizzle about 2 tablespoons of the sauce around each plate; garnish with fresh-snipped micro greens.

SERVES 4

PREP TIPS: Make sure you have a thick kitchen towel or mitten to wear when cooking over very high heat. Also, never lean over the pan while it is hot. When you put the tuna into the pan, always roll it from the front of the pan to the back, and be sure to keep your hand an inch or higher above the pan to avoid getting splattered.

Butcher-cracked pepper is a very coarse grind that you can't get with a standard pepper mill. Use a small spice grinder (or coffee grinder) and just pulse it once or twice. Some people like to put the peppercorns in a plastic bag and smash them with a cast-iron skillet, but the grinder is easier as long as you don't overdo it and end up with a fine grind.

SHOPPING TIP: Block-cut means the tuna is as thick as it is high and wide.

MEAT, GAME, AND POULTRY

Much of the beef the nation consumes is born in Texas and then sent elsewhere to mature and be processed before ending up in those plastic packages in your supermarket. But there's plenty of farm-raised meat and game around, and the flavor of farm-raised meat is much different from that factory package. When cooking these great cuts of meat, I respect the time and love that go into producing them. You may find that your butcher also treats it with great care.

TEXAS PECAN-CRUSTED CHICKEN SKEWERS

TEXAS HONEY MUSTARD LAMB LOIN

with Red Wine–Lavender Jus

The loin of lamb is not often tried by home cooks. It is the most expensive cut of lamb, but it's worth every penny in flavor. That's why I like to enhance it with red wine and lavender, a relative of mint. Lavender is associated with the South of France and is used in many dishes there, so imagine my surprise when I found it growing profusely in Texas Hill Country. I like to cook with the fresh flowers as well as the leaves. Fresh or dried lavender buds are good in salads, dressings, spice rubs, and savory dishes, as well as desserts. But be subtle with lavender, or you will overwhelm the dish, like using too much perfume. (Be sure to buy lavender meant for cooking; don't confuse it with what you get in bath products or incense.) I get lavender from my friends Bunny and Richard Becker, who grow it near their vineyards. This dish matches their wines and lavender, and it pairs well with South Texas ratatouille (see page 90).

Lamb Loin

2 boneless Texas (or other grass-fed) lamb loins,
    about 12 ounces each, trimmed

Salt and freshly ground black pepper for seasoning

1 teaspoon herbes de Provence

1 teaspoon Texas honey (or any unflavored
    good-quality type)

1 teaspoon Dijon mustard

1 teaspoon whole-grain mustard

2 tablespoons extra virgin olive oil

Red Wine–Lavender Jus

1 cup red wine, such as cabernet sauvignon

½ teaspoon fresh Texas lavender buds
    (a little less if using dried lavender buds)
    (see Shopping Tip)

Salt and freshly ground black pepper

1 cup (approximately) demi-glace (see page 140)
    (see Prep Tip)

½ cup micro greens

For the lamb: Combine honey with the mustards and set aside. Cut lamb into 4 equal portions (about 4–5 inches each) and rub each with salt, pepper, and herbes de Provence. To cook lamb medium rare, heat olive oil over high heat in a 12-inch sauté pan until oil is lightly smoking. Reduce heat to medium-high, and cook lamb for 3 minutes on first side. Turn and brush cooked side with some of the honey mustard, and cook for 3 minutes. Turn again, brush with honey mustard, and cook for 15 seconds. Remove meat from pan, cover lightly with tinfoil, and keep warm until ready to serve. Remove pan from heat and skim off any excess fat, then reserve any juice for sauce.

For the sauce: Put the lamb pan over high heat and deglaze with wine. Add lavender buds and lightly season with salt and pepper. Reduce wine to ¼ cup. Add enough prepared demi-glace to the reserved lamb juices (if any) to make 1 cup and return to pan. Cook over medium heat until reduced to ½ cup. Let cool until grease rises to top; skim off grease with a spoon or ladle, and strain the sauce. Keep warm until ready to serve.

To serve: Slice the lamb so that each person has about 6 slices. Fan out the slices on each plate and arrange side dishes, such as South Texas ratatouille. Drizzle sauce around plate and garnish with micro greens.

SERVES 4

SHOPPING TIP: Dried lavender buds are available from shops that carry bulk quantities of herbs and spices. Fresh lavender is often available in farmers' markets and gourmet stores.

PREP TIP: You can use packaged demi-glace concentrate, often stocked with soup mixes, but for the best quality, make your own (see page 140).

ROASTED RACK OF LAMB
with Lemon Thyme Natural Jus and Mint Marmalade

This San Angelo, Texas, lamb rack is a signature dish at the restaurants. For the jus, you will need to buy lamb bones, roast them, then cook them into a sauce. This may sound like a lot of work, but it isn't really, and you can make the sauce the day before you prepare the lamb. The intense flavor and astringency of the dry red wine are neutralized by the sweetness of the Madeira. The mint marmalade is also a key ingredient, because heat and mint create a magical flavor that can become addictive. We usually serve this dish with an organic potato mustard green dauphinois (see page 104).

Mint Marmalade
½ cup Love Creek Orchard jalapeño mint marmalade*
1 teaspoon dried juniper berries
*Substitute mint jelly with ½ finely diced jalapeño added

Lemon Thyme Natural Jus
5 pounds lamb bones (see Shopping Tips)
2 carrots, peeled and roughly chopped
2 medium yellow onions, roughly chopped
2 stalks celery, roughly chopped
1 cup tomato paste
1 cup dry red wine
1 cup Madeira wine

1 gallon water
4 parsley stems (see Flavor Tip)
1 bunch fresh lemon thyme
½ teaspoon lemon zest

Lamb
2 San Angelo lamb racks, Frenched, cut in half and silver skin removed (see Shopping Tips)
Salt and black pepper
1 cup lemon thyme natural jus (from above)

4 tablespoons jalapeño mint marmalade (from above)
4 servings potato mustard green dauphinois (see page 104)

For the marmalade: Toast the dried juniper berries on a sheet pan in a low oven for a few minutes, then grind them to a powder in a spice grinder. In a small bowl, strain the jalapeño mint marmalade and discard the pulp. Add the ground juniper berries; reserve in the fridge.

For the jus: In a 350-degree oven, roast the lamb bones for about 2 hours or until they turn brown (see Prep Tip). Be careful not to let any black spots appear, or the sauce will be bitter. Using some of the fat that comes off the bones, cook the carrots, onions, and celery in a large saucepot until golden brown. Add the tomato paste, and cook until the sauce gets a bit darker. Add the red and Madeira wines, and cook until almost brownish. Add the water and the bones; stir well so that all of the vegetables and tomato paste are well incorporated. Add the parsley stems and lemon thyme, and allow the sauce to lightly simmer for about 5 hours. Remove the bones and vegetables

and add the lemon zest. Continue to cook until it has slowly reduced to a sauce consistency. Strain through a fine-mesh sieve and reserve (in the fridge if you make this a day ahead).

For the lamb: Season the lamb with salt and black pepper; cover the bones with tinfoil. Sear the meat in a hot sauté pan, then finish cooking in a 350-degree oven until it is done to your liking, about 7 minutes for medium rare. Let the meat rest before slicing it into individual chops of 1 or 2 ribs.

To serve: Put some of the potato mustard green dauphinois in the center of the plate, and lean the lamb up against it, showing the cut face. Drizzle the jus and the mint marmalade around the plate and serve hot.

SERVES 4

SHOPPING TIPS: Ask your butcher for lamb knuckle bones or pieces of shank. These are the best for jus. Freeze any leftover bones.

"Frenched" means that the ends of the bones of the rack of lamb are scraped clean and cut slightly at an angle for presentation.

FLAVOR TIP: When making a stock, use the parsley stems, and save the leaves for garnish. Cooking the leaves for long periods, as in stock, turns them bitter.

WARM TEXAS BEEF TENDERLOIN
with Light Soy Vermouth Broth

This beef gets plated before it gets cooked. It is almost like a carpaccio but not quite. Thin strips of beef are warmed with truffle salt right on the plate only until the meat turns blush pink. Then it's quickly brought to the table with a flavorful broth and garnish of beets and fried leeks. We fry leeks in large quantities in the deep fryer, but you can fry up a few in a deep frying pan. Use prime beef for this dish. The tenderloin is so tender that it will slice like butter. The broth should be very thin, just a bit thicker than water.

Leeks
1 leek, julienned
½ cup (approximately) vegetable oil

Broth
2 tablespoons olive oil
1 teaspoon minced garlic
1 tablespoon minced shallots
½ pound button mushrooms, chopped fine
1 cup dry vermouth
2 small cans (14½ oz.) low-sodium chicken broth
2–3 tablespoons soy sauce

Salt and freshly ground white pepper

Beef Tenderloin
7-ounce beef tenderloin
1 tablespoon truffle salt or fine sea salt
   (see Flavor Tip)

1 roasted red beet, sliced about ¼ inch thick
   (see red beet risotto recipe page 8)
Leeks (from above)

For the leeks: Put the julienned leek into an inch of hot oil in a sauté pan. As soon as they are brown, remove, drain on paper towels, and set aside.

For the broth: In a medium-size saucepan, sweat the garlic and shallots in the olive oil. Add mushrooms and lightly salt them to extract their moisture. Cook the mushrooms until all excess liquid has evaporated. Then add the vermouth and reduce by three-quarters. Add the chicken broth and soy sauce, and allow the sauce to cook over a medium heat for about 20 minutes. Taste the sauce and adjust the seasoning with white pepper. You won't need much salt because of the saltiness of the soy sauce. Strain through a fine-mesh sieve and keep hot. Save extra broth for another dish.

For the beef: Slice the beef into small strips approximately 2 inches long, ½ inch wide, and ⅛ inch thick. Arrange 4 or 5 strips on each plate in a circle and season with the truffle salt.

To serve: In a preheated 500-degree oven, bake the plates with the beef for about 30 seconds or until the beef is a light pink color. Remove from the oven; put about 2 tablespoons of the broth in the center of each plate with a slice of roasted beet, and top with the crispy leeks.

SERVES 4

FLAVOR TIP: No longer is there only one type of salt in the kitchen. Cooks are discovering the different textures, colors, and flavors of salts from around the world. Experiment with these and see what fun you can have. For example, sea salt is extracted from the sea (and the expense of doing this is reflected in its cost). Truffle salt is a flavored salt. Most gourmet food stores carry a variety of salts and they can be ordered online, too.

GRILLED SLICED RIB EYE ON TUSCAN BREAD
with Horseradish Mustard Crème Fraîche

Watercress and red plum tomatoes with homemade basil pesto make this open-faced sandwich a popular lunch choice at the restaurants, and sometimes we serve it with afternoon tea. Best of all, it's very easy to eat.

Dressing
½ cup crème fraîche
1 tablespoon whole-grain mustard
½ teaspoon fresh grated horseradish (see Prep Tip)
Salt and white pepper to taste

Salad
2 bunches watercress, washed and dried
1 tablespoon Italian dressing (store bought is fine)

Rib Eye
4 (4-ounce) slices rib eye (see Shopping Tip)
Salt and freshly cracked black pepper
1 loaf Tuscan bread or ciabatta,
       in 4 lengthwise slices
1 teaspoon olive oil
Salt and pepper
4 small red plum tomatoes, sliced
       about ¼ inch thick
4 tablespoons basil pesto (see page 145)

For the dressing: Combine crème fraîche, mustard, grated horseradish, salt, and white pepper in a small bowl; refrigerate until ready to use.

For the salad: Toss the watercress in the Italian dressing and set aside.

For the meat: Season the rib eye with salt and black pepper and place it on a hot grill until desired doneness, about 3 minutes on each side for medium rare. Let meat rest, then slice it about ⅛ inch thick.

For the sandwich: Brush each slice of bread with olive oil, and season with salt and pepper. Grill the bread on both sides, being careful not to burn it. Remove from the grill; spread the horseradish dressing on each slice. Then layer each slice first with the meat, then the tomatoes (season with salt and pepper), and the watercress salad on top.

To serve: Place each open-faced sandwich on a large round plate and drizzle the basil pesto around it.

SERVES 4

PREP TIP: Fresh horseradish root is always better than the stuff in the jar. Peel it like ginger down to the white part, and grate it on the fine side of a box grater.

SHOPPING TIP: Always buy prime-grade rib eye, and ask your butcher to cut it from the more tender front part of the eye. The back part tends to be tough.

FLAVOR TIP: If you can't find crème fraîche you may substitute a good quality sour cream. If you want to duplicate the velvet texture and tangy, slightly nutty taste of crème fraîche, make your own by adding buttermilk to heavy cream and letting it ferment at room temperature for 8 to 24 hours until it is thick. Stir well, cover, and store in the fridge for as long as a week.

JAMIE'S CHILI

This dish is a tribute to my wife, Jamie, whom I met while I was working at The Mansion on Turtle Creek in Dallas. On our first date, we had a chili contest in her apartment complex. I offered to make it with fresh pasta, which I did for the restaurant, but Jamie, a Texas native, thought that was sacrilegious. She never saw kidney beans in chili, either, but I won her over, and it became this thing that we do together whenever we can because it reminds us of our first date. This dish also won first place in a James Beard chili cook-off. Make this chili ahead of time, and use a big pot. Serve it with some fresh crunchy bread and a dark beer such as Shiner bock.

Beans

16 ounces dried kidney beans

6 cups water

3½ teaspoons chile powder

4 ancho chiles, soaked, seeded, and finely diced

1 poblano pepper, seeded and finely diced

2 jalapeños, seeded and finely diced

½ teaspoon onion powder

1 tablespoon garlic powder

½ teaspoon ground cumin

½ teaspoon cracked black pepper

3 or more teaspoons salt

Chili

4 pounds ground beef

1 medium yellow onion, finely diced

2 garlic cloves, minced

1½ pounds canned stewed tomatoes, finely diced

5 ounces tomato paste

2 smoked ham hocks

½ cup shredded cheddar cheese

½ red onion, finely diced

½ cup sour cream

1 diced jalapeño

¼ cup diced fresh tomatoes

Note: Increase or decrease the amounts for these garnishes according to the number of servings.

For the beans: Wash the beans in cold water and drain. Put them in a large bowl with enough cold water to cover the beans, and leave 2 inches of water over them. Soak for at least 8 hours or overnight. Drain the beans; add 6 cups water, chile powder, and ancho chiles, and bring to a boil in a large saucepan. Simmer for 2 hours. Add the poblano, jalapeños, onion and garlic powders, cumin, pepper, and salt. Cover and simmer 3 hours. Cool and refrigerate 6 to 8 hours or overnight.

For the chili: Sauté ground beef in a large dry saucepan until golden brown. Add onions and garlic, and continue to cook until onions are soft. Remove from the stove; drain off excess fat. Add the beef–onion mixture to the beans in a large pot along with the tomatoes, tomato paste, and smoked ham hocks. Bring to a boil, then lower flame to a simmer for 2 hours. (Do not cover the pot.) Adjust seasonings and add water if chili is too thick.

To serve: Spoon the chili into ceramic bowls; garnish each with shredded cheddar cheese, chopped red onion, sour cream, and perhaps some diced jalapeños and fresh tomatoes.

SERVES A CROWD

GRILLED DOUBLE PORK CHOP
with Barbecue Pepper Glaze

The secret to this recipe is the brine. When a pork chop is marinated overnight in a simple brine of sugar and salt, it becomes exquisitely tender. Keep in mind that it's no longer necessary to cook pork to death, so keep it tender and juicy. You'll need to constantly glaze and turn the chops on the grill, but it makes a fun dish for a barbecue served with a whole-grain Dijon mustard sauce and sliced cornichons (similar to our gherkins). Pair it with a dark beer and side dishes such as roasted corn grits and braised mustard greens. It's also good with carmelized fennel tomato ragout (see page 93).

8 double loin or rib pork chops
½ gallon water
1 tablespoon sugar
1 tablespoon salt

Salt and black pepper to taste
1 cup barbecue pepper glaze (see page 141)
4 tablespoons mustard sauce (see page 138)

In a wide deep dish, combine the sugar and salt with water, and mix until they are dissolved. Add the pork chops, and allow them to soak covered in the brine for at least 6 hours, but no more than 24 hours. Remove and dry them off. Season with salt and pepper. Grill the chops for 4 minutes on each side. Then turn them continuously while brushing each side with the barbecue pepper glaze. Continue this process, being careful not to burn them. The glaze will burn easily, so if the pork is not done to your liking, finish cooking the chops in a 350-degree oven. (Meat thermometer should read 130–140 degrees.)

To serve: Place the chops in the center of a large dinner plate, drizzle with mustard sauce, and add two favorite side dishes.

SERVES 4

PAN-SEARED PORK TENDERLOIN
with Jalapeño Cream Sauce

I like the combination of creamy sauce with dry meat, and jalapeño really flavors the pork. Serve this with the Texas-style dirty rice (see page 109) and sautéed haricots verts with shallots and brown butter (see page 95).

Jalapeño Cream Sauce

1 shallot, minced

4 tablespoons vegetable oil

2 ounces cognac

1 cup heavy cream

1 cup demi-glace (see page 140)

Salt and white pepper to taste

1 jalapeño, seeded and minced

Pork

4 pork tenderloins with fat and silver skin removed (see Shopping Tip)

Salt and white pepper to taste

4 tablespoons vegetable oil

Jalapeño cream sauce (from above)

Dirty rice (see page 109)

Haricot verts (see page 95)

For the sauce: In a medium-size pan, sauté the shallots in oil just until they sweat. Deglaze the pan with the cognac (remove the pan from the fire to do this). When flame is out, continue to cook and reduce liquid until it is almost dry. Add the heavy cream and let it reduce by about half. Then add the demi-glace and reduce to a sauce consistency. Season with salt and white pepper. Strain the sauce through a fine-mesh sieve; add the jalapeño. (The longer the jalapeño is in the sauce, the hotter it will become, so time serving according to your heat preference.)

For the pork: Heavily season the tenderloins with salt and white pepper. In a large skillet, sear them in some vegetable oil until they get a deep golden color, about 4 minutes on each side. Finish cooking the pork in a 350-degree oven to desired doneness or until meat thermometer reads 130 to 140 degrees. Let the meat rest for 10 or 15 minutes before slicing into ½-inch-thick pieces.

To serve: On a large round plate, put about ½ cup of dirty rice in the center and haricots verts alongside. Fan out 5 or 6 slices of the pork at the base of the rice, and drizzle the sauce around the pork. Serve warm.

SERVES 4

SHOPPING TIP: One pork tenderloin serves 1 or 2 people, depending on the size of the servings. A 5-inch piece is a good size per serving, so it is possible to make this dish with 2 to 4 tenderloins.

GRILLED CHICKEN BREAST MODENA
with Natural Sage Jus

To me, sage and chicken are like bread and butter, a perfect match. Sage grows all over the country, and, of course, in Texas, so it's easy to get it fresh. Modena, Italy, is where terrific balsamic vinegar is made; we use it to marinate the chicken before grilling. We use "airline" chicken breasts for this but before you turn the page and laugh about airline food, let me explain. This is a style of breast, also called "Frenched," because it has a wing bone still attached for a better presentation. This type of breast actually was served on an airline (in those heady days when flying was fun), and that's where the nickname came from. This is delicious with potato mustard green dauphinois (see page 104), carmelized fennel tomato ragout (see page 93), or haricots verts with shallots and brown butter (see page 95).

Chicken
4 "airline" (Frenched) chicken breasts
½ cup balsamic vinegar
½ cup water
Salt and black pepper to taste

Natural Sage Jus
2 cups demi-glace (see page 140)
12 leaves fresh sage
1 tablespoon unsalted butter
Salt and black pepper to taste

Micro greens

For the chicken: Marinate the chicken breasts in the vinegar and water for 6 hours; save some of the marinade for later use. Pat dry, season with salt and pepper, and brown the chicken breasts on the grill. Continue cooking in a 350-degree oven until done, about 6–8 minutes.

For the jus: Cook the demi-glace with the sage to the boiling point. Add ¼ cup of the reserved marinade, and bring the jus back to the boil. Simmer on very low heat for about 15 minutes. Add butter; season with salt and pepper.

To serve: Put a ring of the potato mustard green dauphinois in the center of a plate. Put the fennel tomato ragout to the side and place a grilled chicken over the gratin. Ladle the natural sage jus over the chicken, and garnish with haricots verts and micro greens.

SERVES 4

TEXAS PECAN-CRUSTED CHICKEN SKEWERS
with Country Gravy

This is an easy dish that is fun to serve to guests who can each have a skewer and dip their chicken in the gravy. You don't need much prep time, either. You simply slide the chicken onto skewers, then dredge the chicken in flour, dip in the egg mix, and finally into the crushed pecans, and bake until done. Make the gravy while the skewers are cooking. The cracked pepper gives the country gravy some texture and a bit of color. You can get bamboo skewers at any Asian market. This is delicious served with Texas-style dirty rice (see page 109) and caramelized fennel tomato ragout (see page 93).

Chicken Skewers

8 (6-inch) bamboo skewers
2 whole boneless, skinless chicken breasts
Salt and black pepper
3 eggs
½ cup milk
1 cup toasted pecans, chopped fine (see Prep Tip page 32)
1 cup flour

Country Gravy

2 tablespoons butter
2 tablespoons flour
1½ cups whole milk
1 tablespoon freshly cracked black pepper

Pinch of salt

Fresh flat-leaf parsley for garnish

For the chicken: Cut each breast in half and remove cartilage. Then cut each piece in half length-wise; season with salt and pepper. Insert the skewer so it goes through the length of each piece of chicken. In a wide shallow bowl (that will accommodate the skewered chicken), stir the eggs and milk with a fork to mix well. Put the flour on a large plate and the pecans on another large plate. Cover the entire piece of chicken with flour, shaking off any excess. Then dip the floured chicken in the egg mixture, again shaking off any excess. Finally, roll the chicken skewer in the pecans, and place skewers on a sheet pan greased with a pan spray. Bake in a 400-degree oven for 10 minutes or until cooked through.

For the gravy: In a sauté pan, melt the butter and stir in the flour until it turns golden brown. Add the milk and black pepper and stir well until all the flour and butter are incorporated into the milk. Cook for about 5 or 10 minutes until the flour taste cooks out. Season the gravy with salt and keep warm.

To serve: On a large white plate, arrange the skewers so they radiate out from the center. Leave enough room in the center for a small bowl of the gravy, so guests can dip their skewer into it. Garnish with parsley.

SERVES 4

GRILLED DIAMOND H RANCH QUAIL
GOAT CHEESE CONTISER, BABY SPINACH,
AND WILD MUSHROOM SALAD
with Toasted Macadamia Nuts and Pomegranate Vinaigrette

I offer my staff $5.00 if they can tell me the meaning of contiser, and so far I haven't lost any money. Nobody can find it in any of our culinary reference books. *Contiser* is a French term that means to put butter or fat under the skin of a bird before cooking to make it moist. Diamond H Ranch in Bandera, the heart of Hill Country, has been supplying us with high-quality farm-raised quail for some time. They raise only as many birds as they can process, trim, and package by hand.

Quail

4 quail, boned and butterfly cut
2 tablespoons fresh goat cheese

Salad

4 cups baby spinach
1 cup wild mushrooms, sautéed
½ cup toasted and crushed macadamia nuts
     (see Prep Tips)
1 pomegranate, cleaned (see Prep Tips)
½ cup pomegranate vinaigrette (see page 144)

For the quail: With your finger rub the goat cheese between the skin and the breast of each quail. Place the quail skin side down on a hot grill for about 2–3 minutes, flip, and grill the other side. It will be medium hot and slightly firm. Set aside.

For the salad: Combine the spinach, sautéed mushrooms, some of the pomegranate seeds, and some of the toasted macadamia nuts. Mix the salad with some of the vinaigrette.

To serve: On an oval plate, pile some salad set just off center, and lean the quail up against it. Garnish the plate with the remaining pomegranate seeds and macadamia nuts, and drizzle some of the vinaigrette around it, about 1 tablespoon per serving.

SERVES 4

PREP TIPS: The best way to get the seeds out of a fresh pomegranate and keep them whole is to cut the fruit in half and scrape out the seeds with a spoon.

To crush the toasted macadamia nuts or most large nuts, simply chop them up with a knife. Using a spice grinder or food processor would make them into a powder.

VEGETABLES AND SIDE DISHES

Side dishes can be the best part of a meal. In my family, once a week we eat only vegetable sides, including whatever seasonal veggies are good and a few different potato, rice, or pasta dishes. With the meat and fish out of the picture, you are forced to expand your repertoire and give vegetables more attention. This is not only fun but healthy. It teaches my kids to appreciate home-cooked meals rather than store-bought or fast foods, and they learn what "farm to table" means. At Las Canarias and Pesca on the River, we have a grand list of sides for lunch and dinner, and even breakfast. We always create these sides in a seasonal way. There is nothing like the taste of local vine-ripened tomatoes compared to those gassed supermarket tomatoes.

SOUTH TEXAS RATATOUILLE

SOUTH TEXAS RATATOUILLE

My late father-in-law, James Brown, grew vegetables on four acres of his south Texas land as a hobby. (He also had about one hundred fruit trees.) One summer day, as I helped him bring in fresh tomatoes, squash, and peppers, I decided to make a ratatouille. For the fun of it, I cut the vegetables into batons rather than the traditional dice. It was such at hit that night with my wife, Jamie, and her parents, Annette and James, that I decided to develop it for the restaurants. It's a great late summer dish using the last of the summer squash, and I love to serve it with lamb. It also makes a terrific main dish with some fresh-baked bread and a glass of wine. Try to cut all of the vegetables into uniform batons, or 2-inch sticks about ¼ inch wide. Except for the eggplant, which will be softer, the vegetables should be al dente. Never overcook this, or it will be mushy. It's best to prepare this in a large shallow, round roasting pan. A wok, especially a flat-bottom wok, would be perfect.

1 large eggplant, cut into batons as described
    above
1 small zucchini
1 small yellow squash
1 small chayote (see Shopping Tip)
½ small jicama
1 small red bell pepper
1 small yellow bell pepper
1 small poblano chile
½ cup extra virgin olive oil

1 white onion, diced
6 medium cloves garlic, minced
4 beefsteak or other ripe tomatoes, diced
½–¾ cup chopped flat-leaf parsley, basil, cilantro,
    and Mexican oregano (see Flavor Tip)
Salt and freshly ground pepper

Sprigs of fresh herbs such as basil, flat-leaf
    parsley, cilantro, and Mexican oregano
    (including the flowers) for garnishing

Cut the eggplant, zucchini, squash, chayote, jicama, and peppers into batons as described above. In a large round pan, sauté onion in olive oil over high heat for about 1 minute, being careful not to burn. Add garlic and cook until very light brown. Continue stirring to prevent burning while adding the eggplant, zucchini, yellow squash, jicama, and chayote. Cook for 3 minutes. Add peppers and poblano and cook for 2 minutes. Finally, add tomatoes and herb mixture and cook for 2 more minutes. Season with salt and pepper. Most of the vegetables should be between al dente and soft, though the eggplant may be a bit mushy.

To serve: Put on plates with prepared lamb, or top with basil leaves or available fresh herbs.

SERVES 8

FLAVOR TIP: Mexican oregano is from the mint family and is similar to marjoram. It is available in Latino groceries and also on the Internet.

SHOPPING TIP: Chayote is a gourdlike vegetable used since ancient times by the Aztecs and widely available today. In France, it is known as christophene, and it has white flesh under a hard green rind. Look for small, firm, unblemished fruit. It can be cooked just like summer squash.

OVEN-ROASTED TOMATOES
with Lemon Thyme

Try this with fresh Roma tomatoes. I get them from Cora at Oak Hill Farms in Poteet. Cora loves farming and is an expert at growing vegetables and fruit for all seasons. Her tomatoes, or "maters," as we say in Texas, are sweet and flavorful. Being from New York, I always thought the nearby New Jersey tomatoes were the gold standard, but I can say these surpass even those. Serve this with sea bass, grilled chicken, or lamb. It is also good tossed with pasta and goat cheese.

12 ripe Roma tomatoes cut into halves
1 tablespoon minced shallots
1 teaspoon minced garlic
2 tablespoons chopped lemon thyme
1 cup olive oil

Preheat oven to 250 degrees. Toss all the ingredients together in a large mixing bowl. Place the tomatoes skin side up on a sheet pan that has 4 sides at least ½ inch high. Pour remaining oil and herbs over them. Roast for about 30 minutes or until they lose some of their moisture and turn slightly dark. Be careful not to burn them.

SERVES 4

CARAMELIZED FENNEL TOMATO RAGOUT

When fennel is in season, I use it with many dishes and find it especially good with fish. The key here is to julienne all the vegetables in lengthwise strips of uniform size. With the olives, simply pit them and slice them in quarters.

2 tablespoons (approximately) vegetable oil

2 medium-size bulbs fennel

1 medium-size white onion

1 medium-size tomato

2 tablespoons minced garlic

3 tablespoons pitted and quartered kalamata olives

2 tablespoons basil, chiffonade

½ teaspoon minced fresh thyme

½ teaspoon ground red pepper flakes

2 tablespoons tomato paste

Salt and black pepper

1 teaspoon sugar

In a large sauté pan, sweat the fennel and onions in the oil at low heat until fully caramelized, about 5 minutes. Add tomatoes, herbs, garlic, olives, and remaining ingredients. Cook another 8 minutes at low to medium heat. Season with a pinch of salt, and add pepper and sugar to taste.

SERVES 4

SAUTÉED ASPARAGUS
and Mimolette Cheese

Standard-size asparagus work best for this, but you can use medium size also. The Mimolette cheese is a change from Parmesan, but you can use Parmesan instead if you wish.

1 bunch or about 20 standard-size asparagus, trimmed 1 inch from bottom

1 tablespoon salt

1 tablespoon olive oil

1 teaspoon minced garlic

Salt and white pepper

¼ cup Mimolette cheese, shaved (see Prep Tips and Shopping Tip)

Cook asparagus in a large pot (see Prep Tips) of salted boiling water until tender, approximately 3–4 minutes. Drain and set aside. In a hot sauté pan, add olive oil and garlic; cook to a golden brown. Toss the drained asparagus in the pan with the oil and garlic, and season with salt and white pepper.

To serve: Arrange asparagus on a plate, and top with shaved Mimolette cheese.

SERVES 4–6

PREP TIPS: Cooking asparagus in a large amount of water allows them to breathe and retain their color.

Shave the cheese with a potato peeler for a nice, consistent look.

SHOPPING TIP: Mimolette is a semihard cow's milk cheese from Lille, France. It has a buttery and nutty flavor and is especially good paired with sherry or port wine.

SAUTÉED HARICOTS VERTS

with Shallots and Brown Butter

I love haricots verts, or French green beans, because they are crunchier than regular green beans. These are blanched quickly, then sautéed briefly with the butter and shallots. They are a perfect complement to chicken and lamb, and I especially like them with wild salmon. If there are any left over, try them the next day for lunch with canned tuna fish.

1 pound fresh haricots verts
1 tablespoon salt
2 tablespoons butter
1 tablespoon minced shallot
Salt and white pepper to taste

In a large pot of boiling salted water, blanch the beans until tender, about 2–3 minutes. Drain and remove to an ice bath, a bowl within a larger bowl of ice to stop the cooking. Allow butter to brown in a hot sauté pan. Add shallots and cook for about 20 seconds or until they begin to sweat. Add haricots verts and sauté for about 2 minutes. Season with salt and white pepper.

SERVES 4

MR. BROOKS' FAMOUS BROCCOLI RABE

Mr. Brooks is actually Wayne Brooks, one of our sous chefs, who likes this recipe so much that he makes it every day, even when it is not on the menu. (He does this when I'm not looking.) I have to admit it is very delicious, especially with fish, or soft shell crab with lemon caper butter.

2 tablespoons butter

3 tablespoons Texas pecans, lightly toasted
   and crushed (see Prep Tip page 32)

1 teaspoon minced garlic

2 teaspoons minced shallots

1 bunch broccoli rabe, cut into 2-inch lengths

2 tablespoons dry white wine

Salt and white pepper

12 pecan halves

In a 12-inch sauté pan, brown the butter and add the crushed pecans, and lightly toss until the aroma is released. Next, add the garlic and shallots; cook until lightly browned. Add the broccoli rabe and toss a few times in the pan to coat it with the other ingredients. Then add the wine and cook over medium heat until wilted, about 4 minutes. Season with salt and white pepper. Garnish each serving with 3 pecans.

SERVES 4

CAULIFLOWER MASHERS
with Mexican Oregano

Guests always ask for this dish, so we cannot take it off the menu. It makes people love veggies, and it's less caloric than potatoes, so it has the blessing of the nutrition police. You may wonder about the butter and cream, but these two fats, though saturated, work to slow down your digestion, and bring more benefit from the vegetable. Everything in moderation! The key is to oven dry the cauliflower before mashing, so it is not watery. You can also make "mashers" with roasted cauliflower and with other vegetables, such as turnips, rutabaga, or broccoli.

1 medium head cauliflower, cut into
    1- to 2-inch chunks
1 tablespoon salt
¼–½ cup heavy cream, heated
1 tablespoon butter at room temperature

4 cloves garlic, roasted to a golden brown
    and pureed (see Prep Tip)
1 tablespoon chopped fresh Mexican oregano*
Salt and white pepper

Cook cauliflower in a large pot of boiling salted water until fork tender, about 15 minutes. Drain it well in a colander, then put the cauliflower on a sheet pan and dry it in the oven for about 2 minutes at 350 degrees. This is an important step, because if there is too much water in the cauliflower, the consistency won't be as good. Put cauliflower, butter, roasted garlic, Mexican oregano, and some of the heated heavy cream into a large bowl; use a stick mixer to combine until the cauliflower is smooth. It should be a bit thinner than traditional mashed potatoes; a consistency the French call pomme puree. Adjust consistency with additional heated heavy cream, and season with salt and white pepper.

To serve: I like to serve this in individual 4-inch iron skillets and sprinkle a few oregano sprigs (or flower buds) on top. You can also put the cauliflower in a pastry bag and pipe it along the edge of the plate, or make a circle on which to place steak or other meat.

*If you are lucky enough to find some oregano that is flowering, snip off some buds for garnish.

SERVES 4–6

PREP TIP: To roast individual garlic cloves, simply toss them unpeeled in some olive oil and place on a sheet pan in a 350-degree oven until golden and soft. If you cut off one end before roasting, you will be able to easily squeeze out the flesh. Mash it with a fork to get a puree.

BRAISED MUSTARD GREENS

There are many wonderful greens to add color to your meals, such as spinach and mustard greens, for which I have a particular fondness. Always rinse fresh greens in a large bowl of cold water 3 times to remove all the sand. Drain off the excess water. Traditionally, greens were cooked in lard for long periods of time, but don't overcook them. They should be just softened. Here is a classic greens recipe that goes with almost any type of meal.

4 slices bacon, diced

¼ pound butter

2 teaspoons minced garlic

½ small onion, diced

1 stalk celery, diced

½ green bell pepper, diced

1 bunch mustard greens, chopped

2 tablespoons apple cider vinegar

2 cups chicken broth

Salt and pepper

In a large pot, cook the bacon in 1 tablespoon of the butter. Then add garlic, onions, celery, and green pepper, and bring them to a sweat. Add the greens and stir so they wilt. Add the vinegar and reduce until it is almost gone. Add the chicken broth and reduce over medium heat, stirring occasionally to make sure the greens don't become dry. When the broth is completely gone, turn off the heat and stir in the remaining butter. Season with salt and pepper.

SERVES 4

SAUTÉED SPINACH
with Garlic Brown Butter

The flavor of spinach is wonderfully set off with butter and seasonings and in some cases with a touch of wine.

2 tablespoons butter
1 teaspoon minced garlic
4 cups spinach with stems removed
¼ cup dry white wine
Salt and white pepper to taste

In a hot sauté pan, allow the butter to brown. Add garlic and cook until golden brown. Add spinach and toss until it begins to wilt. Add white wine and cook until spinach is just soft. Season with salt and white pepper.

SERVES 4

TEXAS HOME FRIES

Texas is famous for its red potatoes that grow in the colder months of January and February. Homegrown local potatoes are sweet and clean tasting. I love to mix potatoes with vegetables in gratins and casseroles. This potato dish is the most popular breakfast side at the restaurant. We like to pair it with our famous migas, a San Antonio specialty: scrambled eggs with diced crisp corn tortillas, serraño pepper, onion, cheese, salt, and pepper.

6 large Texas Red Bliss potatoes, diced but not peeled
1 tablespoon salt
½ yellow onion, diced
½ red bell pepper, diced
2 tablespoons butter
1 tablespoon paprika (see Shopping Tip)
Salt and freshly ground black pepper

In a large pot of boiling salted water, boil the potatoes until barely cooked, about 4 minutes. Drain them well in a colander. In a large pan, sauté the onions and peppers in the butter. Once they are tender, add the potatoes and cook until golden brown. (They will brown faster if you don't move them around too much.) Add the paprika, season with salt and pepper, and serve hot.

SERVES 4

SHOPPING TIP: Paprika is an underestimated spice. I love Spanish paprika, which is used on potatoes all over that country. Paprika can be sweet, mild, or hot. Find one you like, and always get the freshest grind you can find.

GARLICKY GOLD MASHED POTATOES

For this dish, I prefer the texture and flavor of Yukon Gold potatoes. Leave the skin on the potatoes for a healthy and rustic result. Pair it with meat or as a zesty complement to mild-flavored fish.

6 large Yukon Gold potatoes, quartered
1 tablespoon salt
¼ cup roasted garlic puree (see Prep Tip)
4 tablespoons butter at room temperature
½ cup milk, hot but not scalded
1 teaspoon salt or to taste
½ teaspoon white pepper or to taste

Cook potatoes in a large pot of lightly salted boiling water until fork tender, about 20 minutes. Remove potatoes from water, strain in a colander, and dry them off in the oven for about 3 minutes at 350 degrees. With a hand masher (or an electric one), puree potatoes with the roasted garlic, butter, and some of the milk until they become smooth. Adjust the consistency with the remaining milk; season with salt and white pepper. Do not overmix potatoes—3–5 minutes is enough—because they will become gummy. As soon as you add the milk and it is blended, stop mixing.

SERVES 4

PREP TIP: To make a larger amount of garlic puree, trim the top ends of several garlic heads, wrap each in tinfoil, and roast in a 350-degree oven until soft. When the garlic has cooled, simply squeeze the heads to release the garlic, then mash it with a fork. It can be stored in a jar in the refrigerator for a couple of days.

HAYSTACK POTATOES

These are the best fries to have on hand. You can make them ahead and keep them in the freezer, then fry them up quickly whenever needed. They look good on the plate and are good with almost any main dish.

Baking potatoes (Idaho or russet), peeled
Vegetable or canola oil for frying
Salt

Using a mandoline, cut the potatoes into a fine julienne. Rinse them under cold water until water is clear and not cloudy. Steam the potatoes for 4 minutes until partially cooked, and allow to cool. Store in the freezer until ready to use. Cook potatoes in a deep fryer at 325 degrees until crisp and golden brown. Season with salt immediately.

ORGANIC POTATO MUSTARD GREEN DAUPHINOIS

This is served with our roasted rack of lamb (see page 74), and it's my favorite potato recipe. The good news here is that you can make it the day ahead and pop individual servings (or the whole pan) into the oven just before serving. We cut individual rounds for the center of each serving plate.

Mustard Greens
½ bunch mustard greens, rough chopped
2 tablespoons salt (1 for boiling, 1 for ice bath)

Potatoes
½ tablespoon minced garlic
1 tablespoon minced shallot
3 cups heavy cream
Cooking spray or a pat of sweet butter for pan
5 pounds organic Red Bliss potatoes, sliced ⅛-inch rounds
½ pound Manchego cheese, shredded
Salt and pepper

For the mustard greens: Clean the greens and cook them in boiling salted water for about 5 minutes, then shock them in salted ice water. Once cool, remove them from the ice water and let them dry on a clean towel.

For the potatoes: In a medium-size saucepan, sweat the garlic and shallots, then add the cream. Allow to reduce by ½; remove from the heat. Grease the bottom and sides of an 8-inch-square ovenproof casserole with pan spray or some sweet butter. Layer the bottom with potato slices, leaving no spaces. Sprinkle some cheese on top, then some of the greens. Season with salt and pepper, and ladle some of the cream on top of the layer. Repeat this process 3 times. For the top, just do a layer of potato and cheese. Ladle enough cream sauce over the top so that when you press down with the flat of your hand, the cream will come halfway up your fingers. Cover the pan with tinfoil; bake at 350 degrees for about 1–1½ hours. (Check it after 1 hour.) There should be little or no resistance when a knife is pushed down on the dauphinois. Allow it to cool uncovered. Reserve in the fridge.

To serve: Heat the whole pan in a 350-degree oven for 20 minutes. Or, using a circle cutter, take a desired portion from the dauphinois, and reheat it in the oven until the top browns and it's heated through.

SERVES 4

CAVATELLI WITH MIXED TOMATOES
and Sweet Basil Vinaigrette

Small tomatoes of different colors (yellow, red, green) make this a very pretty dish. Serve it for lunch with a salad, or use it as a side dish with fish. We get these tomatoes right off the vine from Oak Hill Farms, so if you have a farmers' market or a garden of your own, keep this recipe in mind, especially if you can get fresh basil, too.

Pasta

1 pound cavatelli pasta (fresh is best, but you
    can substitute dried)
2 tablespoons salt

Sweet Basil Vinaigrette

1 tablespoon minced garlic
2 tablespoons minced shallots
½ cup white wine vinegar
1 cup olive oil

3 pints mixed cherry tomatoes, halved
    (or larger tomatoes quartered)
¼ cup sweet basil, chiffonade

4 basil sprigs
Salt and pepper

For the pasta: Cook the pasta in a large pot of water with 2 tablespoons of salt until al dente, approximately 4 minutes for fresh and 8 minutes for dried. Cavatelli will float when it's done. Drain the pasta, then shock it in ice water so it cools down. Set aside.

For the vinaigrette: In a blender, combine the garlic, shallots, and vinegar. Add the oil slowly while the blender is running to form an emulsion.

For the dish: Put the vinaigrette into a large heated sauté pan. Add the tomatoes and the pasta, and heat through. Season with salt and pepper. Add basil chiffonnade.

To serve: Use wide soup bowls; garnish with basil sprigs.

SERVES 4–6

ROASTED PUMPKIN PINE NUT RAVIOLI
with White Cheddar Cream and Truffle Salt

Pumpkin is always associated with New England and the Pilgrims, but for those of you who don't know, there is a very popular annual pumpkin festival in Texas Hill Country. I like to use fresh pumpkin whenever I can for this dish, but you can use canned pumpkin puree. The "ravioli" is actually made from prepackaged wonton wrappers rather than semolina dough, so this dish is not very difficult to make.

Filling

½ medium-size sugar or pie pumpkin
    (see Shopping Tips)
4 tablespoons molasses
1 teaspoon powdered ginger
1 tablespoon honey
¼ teaspoon allspice
½ teaspoon cinnamon
Salt and black pepper

Sauce

1 teaspoon minced garlic
2 teaspoons minced shallots
2 tablespoons olive oil
½ cup white wine
1 pint heavy cream
½ cup shredded white cheddar
½ teaspoon white truffle oil
Salt and white pepper

Ravioli

1 egg
½ cup milk
1 package 3-inch-square wonton wrappers
    (see Shopping Tips)
1 tablespoon salt

About 2 tablespoons toasted pine nuts
About 2 tablespoons pumpkinseed oil
A few pinches of truffle salt
A few sprigs of micro greens

For the filling: Preheat oven to 350 degrees. Cut the pumpkin in half, then scoop out the pumpkin seeds and membranes. (Discard membranes, but consider roasting the seeds for snacking.) Rub the pumpkin flesh with some of the molasses and all of the powdered ginger. Place both halves face down on an oiled baking sheet and roast in oven for 45 minutes or until soft. Scoop pulp from pumpkin and puree in a blender with remaining molasses, honey, allspice, and cinnamon until smooth. Adjust seasoning with salt and pepper.

(continued)

For the cream sauce: In a hot saucepan, sweat the garlic and shallots in olive oil. Deglaze with the white wine, and reduce until there's only enough sauce to cover the bottom of the pan. Add in cream and reduce to almost a sauce consistency. Remove the sauce from the heat, and while constantly stirring, add in cheese and truffle oil until the cheese has melted. Season with salt and white pepper; strain it through a fine-mesh sieve.

For the ravioli: Whisk together the egg and milk in a small bowl. Lightly brush this egg wash on one side of each wonton wrapper. Put about 1 tablespoon of filling in the center of the wonton wrapper, and fold it in half. With a pair of circle cutters of two different sizes, use the dull edge of the small one to seal in the filling by lightly pressing down on the ravioli, being careful not to cut the wonton wrapper, then use the larger one to cut out your ravioli. Cook the ravioli in a large pot of boiling salted water until they are done. (They will float when they are done.)

Arrange four ravioli on a plate in a desired fashion, such as a tight circle. Drizzle sauce over the ravioli, and garnish the plate with some toasted pine nuts, pumpkinseed oil, truffle salt, and micro greens.

SERVES 4

SHOPPING TIPS: Most pumpkins you find at farm stands and even in the supermarkets are meant for jack-o'-lanterns. These are too stringy for cooking. Buy only sugar or pie pumpkins. Most canned pumpkin puree is as good as what you make from a fresh pumpkin; however, it won't be made from a roasted pumpkin, and that's what gives this dish its special flavor.

Packaged wonton wrappers are available at Asian markets and gourmet stores. If you live in a city with a Chinese neighborhood, buy them fresh.

TEXAS-STYLE DIRTY RICE

Cajuns invented dirty rice made with ground chicken giblets and gizzards, which gave it the "dirty" look. We make it with pork, which gives it more flavor and really complements our pan-seared pork tenderloin (page 83), which is dressed with a jalapeño cream sauce. The combination is dynamite! This is a simple side dish that can pep up a meal. The coffee blackening spice really makes it special.

¼ cup pork sausage meat

½ small onion, diced small

1 celery stalk, diced small

½ green bell pepper, diced small

1 cup white rice (I like Uncle Ben's or any organic brand)

1 teaspoon chopped fresh thyme

½ teaspoon coffee blackening spice (see page 142)

2 tablespoons olive oil

2 cups chicken broth

Cook the sausage thoroughly in a large saucepan before adding onion, celery, and green pepper. Stir frequently; add rice, thyme, and blackening spice. Add the oil to the pan and coat the rice. Add the chicken broth and bring to a boil. Reduce heat to a simmer, cover the pot, and let it cook for approximately 10 minutes. Use a fork to stir it lightly, re-cover, and let cook until rice is tender, about 15 minutes more.

SERVES 4

ROASTED POBLANO AND SWEET CORN RISOTTO

The sweet corn spiked with thyme is the perfect complement to the smoky poblano in the rice. We serve this as a side dish with lamb. (Refer to the red beet risotto recipe on page 8 for a simple way to make risotto ahead of time.)

3 tablespoons olive oil

1 clove garlic, minced

1 shallot, minced

1 cup arborio rice

½ cup white wine

3–4 cups warm corn stock (see page 150)

1 poblano, roasted, peeled, seeded, and diced

3 tablespoons butter

3 tablespoons shredded Parmesan

1 tablespoon salt

White pepper to taste

Fresh cilantro leaves

Heat the olive oil in a large sauté pan, and add the garlic and shallots. Sauté briefly; toss in the rice to coat it in the oil. Then add the wine and allow it to reduce over a low flame while stirring constantly. When the wine is reduced completely, begin adding the corn stock ½ cup at a time, being careful not to let the rice burn. When you have used 2 cups of the stock, add the poblano and continue to add corn stock. Once the rice is cooked and there is no stock left in the pan, add the butter and the cheese. Season with salt and white pepper.

To serve: Put ½–1 cup of the risotto in the center of a small round plate. Garnish with cilantro leaves.

SERVES 4

ROASTED CORN GRITS

Grits are cooked in the same spirit as polenta, creamy and thick. For the ultimate flavor, we add some roasted corn. You will need to roast 3 or 4 cobs of fresh corn and then remove the kernels, and also boil a few cobs and do the same thing. However, the boiled kernels will be pureed, while the roasted ones remain whole and add flavor and texture to the grits. The best way to stir grits (and polenta) is with a wooden spoon.

1 cup roasted corn kernels (approximately
    3 cobs of corn)
2 cups pureed boiled corn (approximately
    6 cobs of corn)
2 tablespoons vegetable oil
4 garlic cloves, minced

3 shallots, minced
9 cups chicken stock (approximate)
1½ pounds dry grits
Pinch of saffron
1 tablespoon salt
Black pepper to taste

For the roasted corn: Roast corn on an outside grill over medium heat until husks are actually black, about 20 minutes. Remove from the fire and peel off husks. Using a 6-inch knife, cut the kernels from the cob and set aside.

For the pureed corn: Boil the husked corn in a large pot of water until tender, about 5–8 minutes. When cool, cut the kernels from the cob and puree them in a food processor.

For the grits: In a large saucepan, sweat the garlic and shallots in the oil. Add half the chicken stock and bring to a boil. Lower the heat to a simmer, add grits, roasted and pureed corn, and saffron. Add the remaining stock slowly while stirring with a wooden spoon until you have a creamy consistency. You may not need all of the stock; it depends on the grits. Cook for 15–20 minutes until soft and creamy. If the grits get "tight," add a little more water or stock. Adjust seasoning with salt and pepper to taste.

SERVES 4

HUITLACOCHE MUSHROOM POLENTA

with Oak Hill Farms Edible Flowers and Manchego Cheese

Edible flowers are underrated. Every year in our gardens, we should grow flowers that we can eat. They're fun. They liven up any plate, whether they are cooked into a dish or served raw as garnish. Always remove all the green stems and leaves from the flowers; then you can julienne the flowers or keep the petals whole. Make enough polenta to serve 8 so that even if you are serving only 4, they can have seconds. It's that good.

1 ounce Texas virgin olive oil (or any high-quality type)

1 shallot, minced

1 clove garlic, minced

½ cup white wine

1 quart chicken stock or broth

1 cup Baretta fine polenta (my favorite, but you can substitute)

4 ounces huitlacoche

1 ounce grated manchego cheese

1 tablespoon whole sweet butter

Salt and black pepper

Put olive oil into a large saucepan over medium heat. Add shallots and cook until translucent. Add garlic and cook 2 minutes without letting the garlic brown. Add white wine and reduce by ½ on high heat. Add chicken stock and bring to a boil. Whisk in polenta with a stiff, long-handle spoon; whip slowly and reduce heat to a low flame. Cook for 5–10 minutes; add huitlacoche. Cook 3 minutes until polenta is smooth. Fold in manchego cheese and butter until completely melted. Add salt and pepper to taste, and set aside to keep hot.

To serve: Small iron side pans or small plates are appropriate for this. Divide polenta into 2–3 ounce portions for 8 people; sprinkle flowers over top.

SERVES 8

HERBED QUINOA

Quinoa has a nutty flavor with a lot of crunch, and it absorbs flavors while cooking and even afterward. I like to serve it with buffalo carpaccio (see page 11).

¾ cup chicken broth
½ cup dry quinoa
Salt and black pepper
1 bouquet garni (see Prep Tip)
1 tablespoon minced fresh basil
½ tablespoon minced fresh tarragon
½ tablespoon minced fresh parsley
2 fresh mint leaves, minced
1 teaspoon lemon mosto oil

In a small saucepan, bring the chicken broth to a boil, then add the quinoa, salt, pepper, and bouquet garni sachet. Cover the pot and cook over low heat until all of the liquid is gone, about 5 or 6 minutes. Uncover the pot, remove sachet, and allow the quinoa to cool before tossing with herbs and lemon mosto.

SERVES 4

PREP TIP: You can make your own bouquet garni by tying some fresh herbs together in a piece of gauze. Parsley, bay leaf, and thyme make the classic bouquet.

DESSERTS

After any delicious and complete meal, people around the table wonder what else they could possibly eat. Dessert is often the highlight of a meal. This is a course with which you can have some more fun and be particularly inspired. When possible, take a break from the meal and have dessert in another room; or shoo guests from the table and give it a new setting and look. Rather than serve coffee or tea with dessert, serve it afterward. A good espresso or tea is a nice finishing touch.

Fortunately, most desserts can be made ahead of time and stored in the freezer or refrigerator only to be assembled at the last minute. Most of these desserts sound a lot more complicated than they really are.

The peach cobbler, spicy pineapple compote, Hill Country cocoa pecan pie, tangerine bread pudding, and chocolate and roasted pepper cheesecake were created by our former pastry chef, Mark Chapman, who was here when this book began. Mark, who is still working in Texas, is one of the country's top 10 pastry chefs according to *Chocolatier* and *Pastry Arts* magazines.

BECKER VINEYARDS RUBY RED GRAPEFRUIT GRANITE

HONEY LAVENDER ICE CREAM

The sight of a field of lavender is wonderful to behold, and the idea of lavender ice cream inspired me in Provence and again in Texas. From the mint family, this herb has spiky flowers and a wonderful fragrance. There is no ice cream as good as your own, no matter what the brand. But once you learn how, ice cream is easy to make. I urge everyone to get a home ice-cream maker.

2 cups milk
2 cups heavy cream
¼ cup Texas (or other high-quality) honey
6 tablespoons sugar, divided into 2 equal batches
1 teaspoon dried lavender buds (available in the bulk spice section)
8 large egg yolks

In a saucepan over medium heat, scald milk, cream, honey, and ½ the sugar. Do not boil. If using a candy thermometer, bring to a temperature of 180 degrees, then remove it from the heat. Add lavender, cover the pot, and allow it to infuse for about 15 minutes. In a large bowl, briefly whisk together yolks and remaining sugar. Gradually whisk milk mixture into egg yolks. Put in a saucepan and cook over medium-high to high heat, stirring rapidly with a heat-resistant rubber spatula, until mixture coats spatula or reaches 180 degrees on a candy thermometer. Do this step as quickly as possible. Immediately strain mixture into a stainless steel bowl, then cool it in ice water for at least 20 minutes. Pour into an ice-cream maker and follow the manufacturer's instructions.

To serve: Scoop into a cocktail glass with cookie garnish.

MAKES 1 ½ QUARTS

BROILED TEXAS RUBY RED GRAPEFRUIT
with Mexican Sweet Chile Salt and Cider Vinegar

Our wonderful Ruby Red grapefruit is not grown in Hill Country, but farther south in the lower Rio Grande valley, where the air is sweet with citrus blossoms every spring. Red grapefruit is only picked when it is ripe, so it is heavy and juicy, with a superior sugar to acid ratio. It is available from November through April and keeps in the fridge for several weeks. This simple broiled grapefruit, sliced into wheels, is a nice way to begin your breakfast, but it also serves as a simple and elegant dessert. You can also make it ahead. Sweet chile salt is a condiment used in Mexico to flavor fruit and vegetables, especially cucumbers.

Chile Salt

3 tablespoons fine sea salt

½ teaspoon sugar

¼ teaspoon cayenne pepper

¼ teaspoon ground lime rind (use a box grater)

¼ teaspoon ground lemon rind

Grapefruit

1 Texas Ruby Red grapefruit

4 pinches Mexican sweet chile salt (from above)

2 teaspoons (approximate) cider vinegar

Fresh raspberries, blackberries, and blueberries for garnish

1 teaspoon julienned mint

For the chile salt: Mix together salt, sugar, cayenne, and citrus rinds; let mixture dry on a sheet pan overnight.

For the grapefruit: Remove skin from grapefruit, and slice grapefruit into ¼-inch wheels. Sprinkle Mexican sweet chile salt over each grapefruit wheel; broil for 1 minute on a sheet pan until slightly warm. Remove pan from broiler, and drizzle cider vinegar over the wheels, about ½ teaspoon each. Cool in refrigerator overnight or for 5 minutes in the freezer.

To serve: Serve grapefruit wheels cold with raspberries, blackberries, blueberries, and mint.

SERVES 4

BECKER VINEYARDS
RUBY RED GRAPEFRUIT GRANITE

These two fruity wines add another dimension to the citrus flavors.

2 cups Becker Vineyards Riesling
2 cups Becker Vineyards port
2 strips of rind each from Ruby Red grapefruit, lime, and lemon
Juice of 4 limes, 2 lemons, 1 Ruby Red grapefruit, and 2 oranges
2 sprigs of Mexican oregano (plus extra for garnish)

Combine all ingredients in 2-quart saucepan and simmer until the alcohol cooks off, about 3–5 minutes. This can be tested by removing the pan from the stove and lighting a match to it. If finished, the alcohol will not flame up. Allow mixture to cool. Remove oregano leaves and strain the mixture. Finely dice the oregano leaves and put them back into the mixture in a shallow pan, and place in freezer. Every hour stir the mixture with a fork. It should fluff up into shiny ice crystals. It's important to stir every hour, for 4–6 hours, until crystals are achieved.

To serve: Serve in a chilled cocktail glass with a few oregano leaves.

SERVES 4

MIXED WILD BERRY SOUP

I like to make this soup in the spring when the dewberries come up in the Hill Country, but you can make it with fresh blueberries.

Sauce

2 cups fresh orange juice

2 slices fresh ginger, peeled

2 tablespoons honey

Soup

4 cups assorted fresh wild berries (blueberries,
    fraise de bois [see Shopping Tip])

1 cup heavy cream

4 cups plain yogurt (nonfat or regular)

6 tablespoons honey

½ cup fresh orange juice

½ cup orange-ginger sauce (from above)

4 teaspoons crème fraîche

Tortilla lattice (optional) (see page 120)

For the sauce: Combine the orange juice, ginger, and honey in a small saucepan. Bring to a boil, lower the heat, and reduce by half. Set aside and allow to cool.

For the soup: In a blender, puree the berries. Add the cream, yogurt, honey, orange juice, and orange-ginger sauce. Puree again. Strain through a fine-mesh sieve and set aside.

To serve: Place 1½ cups soup in each of 6 chilled bowls. Using a squeeze bottle, make a circle of dots with the crème fraîche around the edge of the bowl. Draw the point of a knife through the drops to create a star pattern or swirl. If you use the candied tortilla strips dusted with powdered sugar, arrange them so they stick out of the edge of the bowl. Garnish with fresh berries.

SERVES 6

SHOPPING TIP: Fraise de bois are intensely sweet and very tiny wild French strawberries. They are usually available in specialty stores and sometimes at farmers' markets.

HOT LOVE CREEK APPLE TURNOVERS
with Cranberry Sauce and Mexican Cinnamon

These turnovers are inspired by the apples we get right from the trees at Love Creek Farm. This recipe looks more complicated than it is. You can make the cranberry sauce and the apple filling ahead of time and use store-bought filo (phyllo) dough. Once you get the knack of folding the dough into little triangles, it will take you only a few minutes to prepare the turnovers.

Cranberry Sauce

12 ounces frozen or fresh cranberries

¾ cup sugar

2 cups water

2 teaspoons orange zest

Filling

4 Golden Delicious apples peeled, cored, and diced

Juice of 1 lemon

3 tablespoons butter

½ cup sugar

1 tablespoon applejack (see Flavor Tip)

1 teaspoon Mexican or other high-quality cinnamon

Tortilla Lattice

1 large flour tortilla

Few tablespoons melted butter

Few teaspoons sugar

Turnovers

1 (½-pound) package filo dough (see Shopping Tip)

½ pound (2 sticks) butter, melted

¼ cup sugar

4 ounces crème fraîche

¼ cup powdered sugar

½ cup fresh berries

For the cranberry sauce: Put cranberries, sugar, water, and zest into a medium saucepan, and bring to a boil. Lower heat and simmer for 10 minutes before removing from the stove. Once cool, puree the mixture in a blender, then strain it through a sieve. Return it to the heat, bring to a boil, and continue cooking for 2 or 3 minutes. Cool the sauce and set aside. (It will keep in the fridge overnight.)

For the filling: Toss the diced apples with lemon juice to prevent oxidation. Melt butter in a medium-size saucepan and add the apples, tossing them to coat with melted butter. Cook over medium heat until apples begin to soften, then add the sugar and toss again. Add the applejack and cook until apples are soft and juices evaporate, about 5–8 minutes. Remove from heat and add cinnamon. Set aside to cool. (It will keep in the fridge overnight.)

(continued)

For the tortilla lattice: Preheat the oven to 350 degrees. Brush tortilla with melted butter and sprinkle with sugar. Cut into long, thin strips, and place them on a parchment-lined sheet pan. Weave the strips into 4 lattices, each about 2½ inches square. Trim the ends, and bake lattices until golden brown. (This is optional, but it's easy to make and adds elegance to the presentation.)

For the turnovers: Open the package and lay the filo dough out flat on a cool, clean surface. Cover it with a damp towel to prevent drying. You will need 4 sheets of dough 14×18 inches for each turnover. First, brush 1 sheet with melted butter, and sprinkle with a little sugar. Put another sheet on top, then repeat the process until you have 4 sheets together; do not sprinkle sugar on the top sheet. Trim the edges of the stack and cut 4 equal strips of dough about 4½ inches wide by 14 inches long. Repeat the process until you have 8 strips. Put about 3 tablespoons of filling at the bottom of each strip. Fold the bottom right-hand corner of each strip over to the left to form a triangle. Flip the triangle up and across until you reach the top of the strip. You should end up with 8 turnovers. Place each turnover on a buttered sheet pan; bake at 350 degrees for 20 minutes or until golden.

To serve: Line each plate with cranberry sauce. Put crème fraîche in a squeeze bottle or parchment, and make dots around the border. Use a knife to draw lines through the dots to create heart shapes. Dust the turnovers with powdered sugar; put 2 on each plate. Sprinkle a few fresh berries around the turnovers, and lean a tortilla lattice against them. To create height, place a tortilla strip through a lattice hole.

SERVES 4 (2 TURNOVERS EACH)

SHOPPING TIP: Frozen filo dough, also called phyllo dough, is available in most food stores. It will keep in your freezer for a year, but always defrost it overnight in the refrigerator before using or it will be brittle and may break up during preparation. Fresh filo is usually available in Greek markets and will keep in your fridge for 2 days.

FLAVOR TIP: Applejack is brandy distilled from apples. You can also use Calvados or any apple brandy.

PEACH COBBLER

This is a very easy dessert to make when you have fresh peaches and berries. If not, this is perfectly good using frozen fruit. Serve it warm with vanilla ice cream or whipped cream.

Streusel

1¼ cups brown sugar

1¼ cups sugar

¾ pound (3½ sticks) butter

½ tablespoon cinnamon

½ teaspoon ground black pepper

1 teaspoon salt

2 teaspoons vanilla extract

2¾ cups flour

1¾ cups old-fashioned oats (do not use
  quick-cooking oats)

Filling

6 cups peeled, pitted, wedge-cut peaches

1 cup fresh or frozen blackberries (optional)

1 cup sugar

1 teaspoon vanilla extract

3 tablespoons cornstarch

For the streusel: Put brown and white sugars, butter, cinnamon, pepper, salt, vanilla, flour, and oats into a bowl. Mix together with your hands to form a "crumble" of evenly distributed ingredients.

For the filling: Preheat oven to 350 degrees. Toss together the peaches, berries, sugar, vanilla, and cornstarch in a bowl. Place this mixture in a 9×11–inch buttered baking pan. Top this with ½–inch layer of streusel. Bake until golden brown and bubbling around the edges and in the middle, about 30 to 45 minutes.

To serve: Cut the cobbler into 8 pieces, and top each with vanilla ice cream or whipped cream. Garnish with a few berries.

SERVES 8

SPICY PINEAPPLE COMPOTE
over Coconut-Almond Crusted Ice Cream

This is one of the favorite desserts at Las Canarias and it was a big hit when we prepared it in New York City for a special Texas event at the James Beard House.

2 tablespoons butter

2 tablespoons sugar

2 tablespoons honey

½ lemon, juiced

¼ teaspoon cayenne pepper (more if you like it
    spicier)

¼ teaspoon ancho chile powder

1 fresh pineapple, peeled, cored, and cut into
    small cubes

1 cup toasted, shredded sweetened coconut
    (see Prep Tip)

1 cup toasted sliced almonds (see page 44)

2 pints vanilla bean ice cream

4 dried pineapple chips (see page 152)

For the compote: In a saucepan, heat butter, sugar, honey, and lemon juice, and bring to a boil. Just as the color begins to darken, add the cayenne and ancho chile powder, then lower heat to medium. Toss in the pineapple; continue to cook until the pineapple is heated and glazed. Keep warm until ready to serve.

To serve: Combine coconut and almonds in a bowl. Dip each scoop or serving of ice cream in the bowl, and move it around until it is completely coated. The coating will adhere better if the ice cream is slightly softened. Place the coated ice cream in a bowl or a large martini glass, and pour some hot compote over it. Garnish with a pineapple chip or a fresh pineapple slice cut like a triangle.

SERVES 4

PREP TIP: Buy already shredded sweetened coconut. Spread it on a sheet pan and toast it in a 350-degree oven until browned, no more than 10 minutes.

southern classic. (You can also make up to 8 or 12 individual small pies with this recipe.) Use the best-quality chocolate you can find.

Pie Crust

2¾ cups all-purpose flour, sifted
¼ pound (1 stick) butter
Pinch of salt
3 tablespoons ice-cold water

Filling

½ pound (2 sticks) butter
⅝ cup sugar
¾ cup brown sugar, packed
½ cup honey
¼ cup heavy cream
⅔ cup chopped bittersweet chocolate
1 pound chopped pecans
1 pie shell baked until ¾ done (from above)

For the pie crust: Preheat the oven to 350 degrees. Using your hands, mix the flour with the butter until the fat is dispersed evenly into small pieces about half the size of a pea. Then add cold water and knead it just until it comes together. (Overmixing will make a tough crust.) Wrap in plastic and cool for at least 1 hour. Place chilled dough on a surface lightly dusted with flour. Toss a bit of flour on the pie dough and roll out with a rolling pin to ¼-inch thick. Place in a lightly greased and flour-dusted pie tin. Shape dough to the tin and place parchment paper in the tin; put pie weights (dried beans or rice) over the paper to prevent bottom of shell from cooking. Bake the pie shell until three-quarters done, about 12 minutes. Be sure the dough does not get brown. Remove from oven and allow to cool; remove paper and weights.

For the filling: In a saucepan, bring the butter, sugars, and honey to a rapid boil. Lower the heat and simmer 3 minutes until the mixture bubbles. Add the cream, chocolate, and pecans, and continue to cook and stir until the mixture bubbles again.

For the pie: Pour filling into the pie shell and bake in a 350-degree oven until bubbles appear, about 10–12 minutes. Remove from the oven and chill.

To serve: Serve the pie cold with coffee ice cream and garnish with a chocolate curl.

MAKES A 10- OR 12-INCH PIE

BAYS BAUER TANGERINE BREAD PUDDING

This dessert was inspired by a visit to an orange grove in the Rio Grande valley, where a farmer named Bays Bauer had hybridized a type of tangerine to suit the growing conditions of south Texas. The result is a large, seedless, and wonderfully sweet and tart tangerine. (Substitute large clementines if you cannot get good-quality tangerines.) This is a unique take on bread pudding and was wildly popular at the restaurants because the "bread" is really croissants, which lend a very special flavor to this pudding. For a really good texture to the pudding, first tear the croissants into bite-size chunks, and toast them on a sheet pan in a 375-degree oven.

1 quart heavy cream

½ cup plus 1 tablespoon sugar

9 egg yolks

½ tablespoon vanilla extract

6 cups croissant pieces

8 tangerines, segmented (or 8–10 clementines, depending on size)

1 cup sliced blanched almonds, lightly toasted

4 tablespoons tangerine zest

1 cup half-and-half

Powdered sugar

For the pudding: In a saucepan, warm the cream slightly (about 120 degrees on an instant-read thermometer). Add the sugar and egg yolks, and whisk together until sugar has dissolved. Add vanilla. Then place the mixture in a large bowl along with the croissant pieces, tangerine segments, almonds, and 2 tablespoons of the tangerine zest. Toss lightly until all ingredients are coated. Place the pudding in 6-ounce ceramic soufflé cups (see Prep Tip). Add the half-and-half to each cup, until the cups are three-quarters full. Place the soufflé cups in a baking pan; add water to the pan until it comes about halfway up the sides of the cups. Bake in a preheated 300-degree oven for about 25 minutes or until the custard has solidified. Remove from oven. Cover the pan with plastic wrap to create a steam convection; allow it to cool. This will speed up the cooking process and allow the pudding to cook more evenly.

To serve: Dust each cup lightly with confectionary sugar and serve warm.

SERVES 8

PREP TIP: Instead of individual soufflé cups, you can make this in a 9-inch ceramic baking dish. Cook it another 5 or 10 minutes if you do this.

CHOCOLATE AND ROASTED PEPPER CHEESECAKE
with Rosemary-Scented Cherry Compote

This is a dynamite dessert that combines sweetness with heat and is great fun to serve. We've simplified this to some extent to make it easier for cooking at home—but it may take some practice to get it right. Once you do, however, your dinner party will be the talk of the town. You should have a kitchen scale handy for this, too, because you will need precise measures for the flour, cheeses, and butter. You can make the cheesecake a day or more ahead and keep it in the freezer. You'll need some round rubber molds found in kitchen supply stores, although you can make square or triangular shapes as well. These get baked in a water bath, then put into the freezer until you're ready to assemble the dessert.

Cheesecake

¾ cup sugar

12 ounces cream cheese

10 ounces mascarpone cheese

3 eggs

½ cup chopped semisweet chocolate

¼ cup cream

1 tablespoon melted butter

½ roasted poblano pepper, pureed

⅛ teaspoon cayenne

Toasted Walnut Base

7 ounces butter

½ cup sugar

2 eggs

7 ounces all-purpose flour

1 tablespoon vanilla

2 tablespoons chopped toasted walnuts

Compote

1 ounce butter

2½ tablespoons sugar

1 tablespoon honey

1 tablespoon lemon juice

½ sprig fresh rosemary, wrapped in cheesecloth

¾ cup pitted cherries (see Shopping Tip)

1 teaspoon cornstarch

1 tablespoon water

Shaved chocolate for garnish

(continued)

For the cheesecake: In a mixing bowl with a paddle attachment on low speed, blend sugar, cream cheese, and mascarpone until smooth. Set to medium speed, then add eggs 1 at a time. Put the chocolate into a bowl. In a saucepan, bring cream to a boil; pour it over the chocolate, and whisk to make a ganache. Slowly pour some of the cheese mixture into the chocolate to cool it without "cooking" the eggs in the cheese mix. Fold in the melted butter, poblano, and cayenne, then fold it all into the cheese mixture, using the paddle until fully incorporated. Put into round molds in a baking pan with water, and bake in a preheated oven at 300 degrees with water bath for 20 minutes. Cool and freeze.

For the toasted walnut base: Cream the butter and sugar; add eggs slowly, followed by the flour, vanilla, and nuts. Pour into a 9×11-inch pan, and bake at 325 degrees about 10 minutes until ¾ cooked. Reserve.

For the compote: Melt the butter; add the sugar, honey, and lemon. Drop in the rosemary and slowly simmer to allow the rosemary to steep. Then add cherries and continue cooking until the compote bubbles. Mix the cornstarch with 1 tablespoon of water to form a slurry. Add it to the compote; continue to cook until it thickens, about 2 minutes.

To serve: Cut the walnut base into rounds the same size as the cake molds. Place each slice on a large dessert plate and microwave for 15 seconds. Remove cheesecakes from freezer, pop them out of their molds, and defrost for about 30 minutes. Place each cake on top of the base and pour about 3 ounces of the warm cherry compote in front of the round. Garnish with a chocolate curl or stick.

SERVES 8–12

SHOPPING TIP: Use fresh cherries or *griotes,* which are cherries marinated in brandy. You can find them frozen in gourmet food stores. They are not maraschino cherries.

FROM THE CHEF'S PANTRY

Consider this chapter your pantry of sauces, vinaigrettes, demi-glace, stock, and garnishes to use in many of the dishes in this book, and with your own favorite recipes. Here also are some ideas about equipment, techniques, and presentation I've developed over the years that may help make your culinary life more fun.

What Really Matters: Equipment You Need—
and Don't Need

Many cooks like to chop everything by hand because they enjoy the process and the pure sensual pleasure of working with food. Others fall in love with every gadget that comes along—and with the burgeoning interest in all things culinary, there are many temptations in the kitchen supply stores and catalogues.

There are some gadgets I do like, such as a French mandoline for slicing shoestring fries, shaving fennel, and making otherwise fancy or paper-thin cuts. (The Japanese mandoline is less expensive and also good.) But the most important tools are good knives. I use 6-inch and 8-inch chef's knives (also known as French knives), a boning knife, a paring knife, and a serrated bread knife. I also have a long beveled knife that's great for slicing everything from meat to cheese to veggies. The bevels create air pockets and eliminate drag. If you plan to serve sushi or tartare often, then it would pay to invest in a sushi knife. It's also a good idea to have a diamond knife-steel (with a hand guard) to keep your knives sharp.

I like cast-iron skillets, as well as heavy-duty nonstick pans for high heat searing without the potential for burning. A wok is also useful for sautéing large amounts of food on a stove top, such as ratatouille.

A mini-coffee grinder is really important for grinding spices and herbs, especially for cracking black pepper. A box grater is all you need to shred cheese and other foods. The inexpensive old-fashioned potato peeler is the best kind. The newer ones take too much skin off the fruit or vegetable. Peelers are also useful for zesting a lemon or other citrus fruit.

Have two spatulas: a regular offset spatula for meats and a thinner, more flexible spatula for fish. This type glides under the fish or other delicate food without breaking it. I have to admit I like tongs, but anyone who brought tongs into a French kitchen would be called an idiot and demoted to short order cook. Also, a meat fork that looks sort of like a tuning fork comes in handy.

A blender or food processor is useful and also a hand blender that you put right into the pot to puree a soup. Most chefs (and foodies) refer to them as stick mixers.

For presentation, keep several sizes of ring molds on hand, such as a 3-inch ring to shape and center a salad or tartare portion on a plate with other food. Ask your plumber (or, if you're handy, do it yourself) to cut some molds from PVC pipe in different widths and heights. These are easy to keep clean and will last forever. But you can't use them for hot food or anything that goes in the oven. For that you need stainless steel. Rubber molds in various shapes come in handy, too, for a variety of desserts, salads, and other foods. They are used for baking and freezing. Small iron skillets (4- or 6-inch diameter) are handy for presentations of individual quiche or side dishes.

Some Sleight-of-Hand Techniques for Culinary Magic

OVEN-DRYING: For pure flavor and undiluted texture for mashed potatoes and other vegetables, always dry them out on a sheet pan in the oven for a few minutes before mashing. It makes a very big difference.

SHAVING: When you want paper-thin slices of raw fish, you need to "shave" it with an extremely sharp sushi knife. I prefer this technique over chopping for making tuna tartare and similar dishes because you are saving the natural oils in the food, whereas grinding or chopping them releases these oils and the result is less flavor.

SEASONING WITH SALT AND PEPPER: Throughout the book, we've left the amounts of salt and pepper for seasoning up to the cook because this is such an individual taste. However, one strict rule I have is that when you deep fry foods, season them immediately after frying with salt and pepper. Seasoning them after they have cooled off—even for a few seconds—prevents the salt and pepper from getting to the food. All it does is stick to the outside coating.

Plating and Presentation with Style

Our eyes are the windows not only to our soul, but to our appetites. When food is beautifully presented, we're hooked. It tells you the cook has put lots of love and care into preparing it. The Japanese have known this for centuries and consider each plate (or bento box) a complete work of art. In recent decades the rest of the culinary world has caught up with them, and one of the most important parts of my work is making sure the presentation lives up to the food itself. I have lots of fun thinking up new ways to present food. However, my first concern always is the taste. If food doesn't live up to taste standards, then all the fancy plating in the world isn't going to help.

I'm a fan of good-quality china, elegant white plates. It's the canvas, and the food is the art. My favorite china is Villeroy & Boch. Glass plates can also add some depth to your collection. Naturally, size and shape matter, so that the food and plate are in the right proportion. With the emphasis on small plates these days, you may want to acquire extra sets of small plates along with the larger ones—square, oval, round. Try serving in a vessel that doesn't normally go with the food. For example, maybe you have some beautiful demitasse cups you rarely use. Why not serve a chilled soup appetizer in them, or use a tall glass to serve gazpacho? And who hasn't had a passed canapé served in a porcelain Asian soup spoon? I like to serve ceviche in a large margarita or martini glass or on a glass plate.

The way food is arranged on the plate and garnished is fun, and it's why I've tried to suggest ways to do this with each recipe. With a bit of practice, you'll get the hang of garnishes, too. You can drizzle a colorful oil or dressing around the plate with a spoon.

SMOKY TOMATO SAUCE

Next time you are grilling with wood, make a batch of this sauce. It's good on any fried meat or fish, and it will keep for a week in the refrigerator. I keep smoked tomatoes in the freezer for easy access. This is a thick sauce, like marinara.

6 Roma tomatoes, washed and cored
¼ cup roughly chopped yellow onion
1 teaspoon minced garlic
1 tablespoon olive oil
¼ cup balsamic vinegar
1 teaspoon salt or to taste
½ teaspoon pepper or to taste

Smoke the tomatoes for 15 minutes over mesquite or apple wood, then rough chop them. In a medium saucepan, sweat the onions and garlic in the olive oil. Add the tomatoes and vinegar. Stir continuously and simmer for 5 minutes over medium heat or until the liquid has reduced. Remove the tomatoes from the heat and puree in a blender. Adjust the seasoning with salt and pepper, and thin with water if needed. Caution: Let the tomatoes cool, or keep the lid on the blender so hot food doesn't touch you.

MAKES ABOUT 2 CUPS

SPICY TOMATO COULIS

This is a medium-thick sauce, thinner than the smoky tomato sauce. I use it with the buffalo carpaccio, but it is also good on a sandwich as a replacement for mayonnaise. It is a good dipping sauce on antipasto platters and even with hard cheeses. Try it with pita bread instead of hummus.

1 tablespoon olive oil
2 tablespoons minced garlic
1 tablespoon minced shallot
½ serraño pepper, minced
1 teaspoon chile powder
4 Roma tomatoes, rough chopped
3 tablespoons tomato juice
Salt and black pepper

In a medium-size saucepan with 1 tablespoon olive oil, sweat the garlic, shallots, and serraño. Add the chile powder and lightly toast it for about 10 seconds. Add the tomatoes and cook them until they begin to break down. Then add the tomato juice, and season with salt and pepper. Allow the liquid in the pan to reduce until it is almost dry, about 4 minutes. Puree the mixture in a blender and then strain through a fine-mesh sieve. Use the back of a spoon to push the solids through the strainer until there is only a dry mass left, or the coulis will be runny. This keeps in the fridge for 2 or 3 days.

MAKES ABOUT 1 CUP

WATERCRESS SAUCE

This cold green sauce is served with our buffalo carpaccio, but it also pairs well with fish, especially salmon.

2 tablespoons mayonnaise
2 tablespoons crème fraîche
½ lemon, juiced
¼ teaspoon salt or to taste
Pinch of cayenne pepper
1 cup watercress (use hydroponic for fewer stems and more flavor)

In a medium-size bowl, mix the mayonnaise, crème fraîche, lemon, salt, and cayenne; set aside. Remove any stems from the watercress and puree in the food processor. Begin on medium speed, then turn to high. If necessary, put a little bit of the mayonnaise–crème fraîche mixture into the processor to get the watercress going. Strain the watercress through a fine-mesh sieve, and combine it with the mayonnaise and other ingredients.

MAKES ABOUT 1 CUP

WHOLE-GRAIN DIJON MUSTARD SAUCE
with Sliced Cornichons

This sauce is served with our double pork chop (see page 82), but it works with grilled or roasted chicken, pork, or veal, and with grilled tuna or similar steaklike fish.

1 cup heavy cream
1 cup demi-glace (see page 140)
1 tablespoon whole-grain mustard (French brands are best)
1 tablespoon Dijon mustard
3 tablespoons sliced cornichons
Salt and white pepper

Reduce the cream in a saucepan until it begins to thicken. Add the demi-glace and reduce until it has a nice sauce consistency. Add the mustards and cornichons; season with salt and white pepper. Cook until warmed through.

MAKES ABOUT 2 CUPS

ROASTED RED PEPPER SAFFRON ROUILLE

This is a hot rust-red colored sauce used in the classic bouillabaise (*rouille* means "rust"). It's often mixed with fish stock, and it's sometimes served as a garnish with fish and fish stews.

2 egg yolks
Pinch of saffron
2 cloves roasted garlic (see Prep Tip on page 98)
Juice of ½ lemon
¼ roasted red pepper
2 ounces vegetable oil
Salt and black pepper

In a blender, puree the egg yolks with the saffron, garlic, lemon juice, and red pepper. Slowly drizzle in the vegetable oil until emulsion forms a mayonnaise consistency. Season with salt and pepper. This will keep a day or two in the fridge.

MAKES ABOUT ⅔ CUP

Demi-Glace, Glazes, and Rubs

DEMI-GLACE

Demi-glace is the foundation of many sauces, an intense concentration of meat stock, seasonings, and wine reduced until it is a thick glaze that coats the back of a spoon. It is the base of many other sauces for meat requiring a brown sauce. Most demi-glace is made with veal bones, but if you make your own at home, it's much easier with chicken bones. Whenever you cook chicken, just keep storing the bones in the freezer until you have enough.

5 pounds chicken bones (necks, wings, backs)
1 teaspoon kosher salt
1 teaspoon cracked black pepper
¼ cup olive oil
1 carrot, chopped
1 onion, chopped

2 celery stalks, chopped
3 sprigs fresh thyme (or ¼ teaspoon dried thyme)
3 sprigs fresh rosemary (or ¼ teaspoon dried rosemary)
1 (6-ounce) can tomato paste
Water

Preheat oven to 450 degrees. Season the chicken bones with kosher salt, freshly cracked black pepper, and olive oil. Put them into a roasting pan with sides 5 or 6 inches high and roast in oven until the bones begin to brown, about a half hour. Then add the carrot, onion, celery, thyme, and rosemary, and roast for another half hour. Add tomato paste and roast another 15 minutes. Add water to cover the bones and come within ¼ inch of the top of the pan. Reduce oven heat to 375 degrees and roast 2 more hours. Discard the bones and strain the juices through a sieve. Then put this into a sauté pan and reduce it on the stove until it thickens to a jelly-like consistency.

MAKES ABOUT 2 CUPS

BECKER PORT GASTRIQUE

A *gastrique* is a syrupy reduction of caramelized sugar and vinegar, sometimes with fruit added. It balances tart and sweet flavors as a base for sauces for duck, game, and game birds. I modernize it by using port wine as the fruit.

2 cups Becker Vineyards port
1½ cups balsamic vinegar

In a small saucepan, combine the wine and the vinegar; reduce over medium heat until mixture thickens. During the reduction, skim the foam off the top of the gastrique in order to get a good, clean-looking sauce.

MAKES ABOUT ½ CUP

BARBECUE PEPPER GLAZE

This glaze was developed for the double pork chop on page 82, but it is delicious with any barbecued meat, as well as with grilled vegetables.

2 tablespoons butter
1 shallot, minced
1 clove garlic, minced
1 tablespoon chile powder
1 teaspoon cumin powder
¼ cup apple cider vinegar
½ cup orange juice

3 tablespoons dark brown molasses
2 tablespoons dark brown sugar
1½ cups ketchup
2 tablespoons freshly cracked black pepper
Dash of salt
Pinch or 2 of cayenne pepper

Sweat the shallot and garlic in the butter in a medium-size saucepan. Add the chile powder and cumin. Allow the spices to lightly toast, then add the vinegar. Reduce by half, then add the orange juice. Reduce again by half; add the molasses and sugar. Stir until all the sugar has dissolved, then add the ketchup and black pepper. Let the sauce simmer over a low heat for about 20 minutes; season with the salt and cayenne. The longer the cayenne is in the sauce, the hotter the sauce will be.

MAKES ABOUT ⅔ CUP

COFFEE BLACKENING SPICE

Make a batch of this to keep on hand. We add this mix to our Texas-style dirty rice (see page 109), and it is a delicious rub for grilled meats, vegetables, or any number of things.

2 tablespoons high-end coffee, ground fine
2 tablespoons cocoa powder
2 tablespoons cayenne pepper
2 tablespoons onion powder
2 tablespoons garlic powder
2 tablespoons dried thyme
2 tablespoons paprika
2 tablespoons dried basil

Mix everything together and store in a glass jar for a few weeks. (The coffee will lose some of its flavor if kept too long.)

MAKES 1 CUP

Oils, Vinegars, and Dressings

CHIVE OIL

We use this to garnish tuna tartare (see page 24), but you can use it to spice up any plate with fish or meat. Decorate the plate by drizzling some from a spoon. Combine a small bunch of chives with safflower or grape seed oil in the blender until the oil is green. This will keep in the fridge for a week.

MAKES ABOUT 1–2 CUPS, DEPENDING ON AMOUNT OF OIL USED

CHILE OIL

We garnish our chile-spiked Mexican shrimp appetizer (see page 14) with this oil, but you can keep it on hand for a variety of dishes that need a bit of heat and some color.

1 cup sunflower or saffron oil
2 tablespoons chile powder

Stir the chile powder into the oil; let it infuse at room temperature for 1 day before refrigerating. It will keep for 3 or 4 days. The longer you keep it, the more intense the color will get.

MAKES 1 CUP

RED PEPPER JALAPEÑO VINEGAR

We use this spicy vinegar on our fried calamari, but it is a flavor complement on any fried fish or chicken.

½–1 jalapeño pepper
1 tablespoon butter
½ cup sushi vinegar (this is a bit sweeter than rice wine)
1 tablespoon crushed red chile flakes

Finely dice the jalapeño, keeping the seeds, and sauté it slowly in butter until it is soft. This is a *brunoise*. In a small bowl, combine this with the vinegar and chile flakes. Serve the sauce in individual ramekins.

MAKES ½ CUP

HUITLACOCHE VINAIGRETTE

This vinaigrette is used on shrimp, and it makes a great cocktail sauce instead of the regular tomato type.

1 6-ounce can huitlacoche (available from Latin grocery stores)
¼ cup rice wine vinegar
1 tablespoon chopped fresh cilantro
¼ cup olive oil
1 teaspoon salt
½ teaspoon black pepper

In a blender, puree the huitlacoche, vinegar, and cilantro. Slowly add oil; season with salt and pepper. For a smoother vinaigrette, put it through a fine-mesh sieve. This is optional, however, because some prefer a rough texture. Use this the same day you make it or you will lose much of the fresh cilantro flavor.

MAKES 1 CUP

POMEGRANATE VINAIGRETTE

This dressing is served with the spinach and wild mushroom salad that accompanies our Diamond H Ranch quail (see page 86). Try it with any salad of fresh greens.

¼ cup red wine vinegar
¼ cup pomegranate concentrate
1½ tablespoons sugar
½ shallot, minced
1 egg yolk
½ cup vegetable oil
Salt and white pepper

Combine the vinegar, pomegranate concentrate, sugar, shallot, and egg yolk in a blender. With the blender running slowly, add the vegetable oil; season with salt and white pepper. This will keep a day or two in the fridge.

MAKES 1 CUP

BUTTERMILK DRESSING

This dresses the greens with our grilled ham and cheese sandwich on page 52, but it's delicious with many types of salads and sandwiches.

½ cup sherry vinegar
½ cup extra virgin olive oil
2 cups buttermilk
2 tablespoons Dijon mustard
Salt and black pepper
6 drops lemon juice

Mix everything together in a blender or in a bowl with a whisk.

MAKES ABOUT 3 CUPS

BASIL PESTO

We use this to garnish our grilled rib eye sandwich (see page 78), but it is perfect for hot or cold pasta, or use it on a salad with a pinch of vinegar.

1 cup fresh basil leaves
½ cup Parmesan, grated
¼ cup pine nuts, toasted
¼ cup olive oil
Salt and black pepper

Pulse the basil, Parmesan, and pine nuts in a food processor. Slowly add the oil until well blended; season with salt and pepper.

MAKES ABOUT ½ CUP

CILANTRO ANCHO CHILE REMOULADE

This dressing is served with our crab cakes (see page 22), but it is good with any chilled poached seafood, on a sandwich, or with fried soft-shell crabs.

1 cup mayonnaise

1 tablespoon drained and finely chopped capers

1 tablespoon finely chopped cornichons (or gherkins)

2 tablespoons chopped fresh flat-leaf parsley

1 teaspoon Dijon mustard

1 anchovy fillet, minced

1 teaspoon Worcestershire sauce

2 teaspoons ancho chile paste

1 tablespoon finely chopped fresh cilantro

Salt and black pepper

Mix everything together in a medium bowl, season with salt and pepper, and refrigerate.

MAKES ABOUT 1¼ CUPS

GRILLED PINEAPPLE SERRAÑO SALSA

We use this salsa with our oyster appetizer (see page 20), but it's good with just about every meat or fish dish, especially a grilled steaklike fish.

1 pineapple, peeled and cut into ¼-inch slices
1 serraño pepper, seeded and finely diced
½ red bell pepper, finely diced
¼ small red onion, peeled and finely diced

½ bunch cilantro, minced
1 teaspoon sugar
1 tablespoon rice wine vinegar
Salt and black pepper

Grill the pineapple slices on both sides, cool them off, then dice them. Put them in a bowl, and add the peppers, onion, cilantro, sugar, and vinegar. Season with salt and pepper.

MAKES ABOUT 4 CUPS, DEPENDING ON SIZE OF PINEAPPLE

BLACK BEAN SALSA

This is served as a garnish with our black bean soup (see page 28). You can serve it with fish such as sea bass or all by itself with a bowl of tortilla chips.

½ pound dry black beans, soaked and cooked
   (see page 29)
1 red bell pepper, seeded and finely diced
1 yellow bell pepper, seeded and finely diced
1 poblano pepper, seeded and finely diced
1 jalapeño, seeded and finely diced
1 red onion, peeled and finely diced
1 red tomato, finely diced

1 yellow tomato, finely diced
1 clove garlic, minced
1 bunch cilantro leaves, chopped
½ cup fresh lime juice
¼ cup olive oil
Salt and black pepper

Combine all ingredients, including the beans, and adjust the seasonings. Marinate overnight.

MAKES ABOUT 4 CUPS

ROASTED CORN RELISH

This is the best corn relish in the world! I've been perfecting it for many years, and I challenge even the likes of Chef Bobby Flay, the guru of Southwestern cuisine. We serve it here with crab cakes (see page 22), and it is good with many other dishes. Also try it with fajitas in place of guacamole.

½ cup finely diced red onion

½ cup seeded and finely diced red pepper

½ cup seeded and finely diced poblano pepper

¼ cup vegetable oil

4 ears fresh corn, roasted, and kernels removed
   from cobs (see page 111)

2 tablespoons cider vinegar

Salt and black pepper

½ bunch cilantro, chopped

In a hot sauté pan, sweat the onions and peppers in the vegetable oil. Add in the corn, and deglaze the pan with the cider vinegar. Season with salt and pepper. Allow to cool. Then add the cilantro.

MAKES ABOUT 3 CUPS

PICKLED RED ONIONS

These are served with baby iceberg lettuce salad (see page 44), but pickled onions are perfect as a garnish, on a sandwich, or as a table condiment. You can double or triple this recipe to make more and keep them in the refrigerator.

1 teaspoon mustard seeds

½ cup red wine vinegar

¼ cup sugar

½ red onion, julienned

In a medium saucepan, toast mustard seeds. They will begin to pop when they are properly toasted, so be careful or they will jump out of the pan. Add the red wine vinegar and sugar; bring to a boil. Pour over red onion and allow to sit for at least 2 hours. You can refrigerate this for 1 week.

MAKES ENOUGH TO GARNISH 4 SALAD SERVINGS OR SANDWICHES

Other Sauces

MINT POTEET STRAWBERRY CONSERVE

I make batches of this when the Poteet strawberries are ripe. The chopped dried strawberries add more texture to the conserve. This is an excellent accompaniment to many meat dishes, but it's also delicious slathered on a piece of fresh bread.

1 teaspoon minced fresh ginger

1 teaspoon minced shallot

1 teaspoon butter

Approximately ¼ to ½ teaspoon salt or to taste

1 teaspoon coarsely ground black pepper

1 cup roughly chopped dried strawberries

2 cups Becker Vineyards port

1 pint fresh Poteet or local strawberries, hulled and cut in half

1 tablespoon fresh mint, chiffonade

In a medium-size saucepan, sweat the ginger and shallot in butter; season with the salt and black pepper. Add the dried strawberries and deglaze the pan with the port. Bring the port to a simmer, and allow it to reduce by half. Then add the fresh strawberries and cook until almost all of the liquid is gone. Let the conserve cool, then stir in the mint chiffonade.

MAKES ABOUT 1–1 ½ CUPS

CORN STOCK

This is the stock to use with the risotto on page 110. Also use it for corn chowder, vegetarian soups, or any recipe that calls for a white stock. You can keep this in the freezer to have on hand when you need it.

6 ears sweet yellow corn

1 teaspoon minced garlic
2 tablespoons butter
1 small yellow onion, roughly chopped

2 stalks celery, roughly chopped
1 carrot, peeled and roughly chopped
½ gallon water
1 bunch fresh thyme
1 bay leaf

For the corn: Remove the kernels from the corn cobs by putting the wide end of the cob on a cutting board and cutting straight down all sides. Reserve corn and the cobs in the fridge.

For the stock: In a large pot, briefly cook the garlic in butter. Add the onions, celery, and carrots, and heat through. Add the water, herbs, and the cobs; cook for 45 minutes. Once the stock is cooked, strain it, then add kernels of corn. Puree the stock; put it back on the heat and allow it to simmer for at least 10 minutes. Remove from heat and reserve.

MAKES ABOUT 1–1½ QUARTS

Garnishes

CANDIED GRAPEFRUIT ZEST

This is a lovely garnish for almost anything, from ceviche to sashimi to topping off game dishes.

3 grapefruits
½ cup sugar
1½ cups water

Julienne the zest of 3 grapefruits. Put ½ cup water into each of 3 small saucepans on the stove. Put ½ cup sugar in 1 pot. Bring all 3 pots to a boil over medium-high heat. When the pot with the sugar boils down to a simple syrup, remove it from the heat and set aside. Blanch the zest in the remaining 2 pots for a few minutes until it softens. Use a slotted spoon or small strainer and dip it first in 1 pot of boiling water, then the other. This double dipping will eliminate all of the bitterness in the zest. Put the blanched zest into the pot with the simple sugar and allow it to cool. This will keep in the refrigerator for two weeks.

MAKES ENOUGH FOR ABOUT 12 GARNISHES

APPLE CHIPS

You may need only a few of these chips for garnish, but you can make a larger amount and store them in a dry place.

1 Granny Smith apple, sliced paper thin
1 quart water
1 cup sugar

Boil the sugar and water to dissolve the sugar. Remove from heat and allow it to cool or chill it in the fridge, then dip the apple slices. Place them on an oil-sprayed cookie sheet. Dry in a 200-degree oven for a total of 8 hours: 4 hours on each side or until crispy. This is much simpler if you happen to have a home dehydrator.

MAKES 12 CHIPS, DEPENDING ON THE SIZE OF THE APPLE

PINEAPPLE CHIPS

These are the garnish for our spicy pineapple compote on page 124, but you can use them for other desserts, salads, or wherever you like. Increase the amounts to make larger quantities of chips.

4 extra-thin slices fresh pineapple
4 teaspoons sugar

Lightly sprinkle sugar over pineapple slices. Place on a nonstick surface in a 225-degree oven for several hours until dry and crisp. Cut or break into chips. Store in a container in a cool, dry place. Chips will keep indefinitely.

MAKES ABOUT 20 CHIPS

SWEET POTATO CRISPS

We use these easy chips to make crisps as a garnish, but if you are going to heat up a pot of oil, then you will want to serve them as a side dish.

1 large peeled sweet potato, julienned
1 quart peanut oil for frying
Salt to taste

In an electric fryer or large saucepot, heat oil to 350 degrees. Using a mandoline or with a sharp knife, make very fine, long julienned strips. Place sweet potatoes in a fryer until bubbling stops, but don't let them get brown. Remove to a perforated pan to drain; immediately season with salt to taste. Reserve at room temperature.

MAKES ENOUGH FOR 2 SIDE DISHES OR AS GARNISH FOR 6-8 DISHES

PARMESAN TUILE

Tuile is a French word for a special cookie that is placed over a mold when it is hot from the oven to form a "tile." We make these with Parmesan and use for garnishing the crispy skin red snapper cioppino on page 66 and also some salads. The flour takes the moisture from the cheese so that you get a nice crisp *tuile*. This recipe makes 8 *tuiles,* but to increase amounts just keep the 4 to 1 ounce ratio of cheese to flour the same. (Do not add any salt as the cheese is already salty.)

4 ounces freshly grated Parmesan
1 ounce all-purpose flour (2 tablespoons)
Pinch of freshly cracked black pepper
PAM spray to grease pan

Spray PAM on a sheet pan and preheat the oven to 350 degrees. Toss the Parmesan, flour, and pepper together and form small rounds ¼-inch high and about 4 inches in diameter. Bake until the cheese melts, about 5 minutes. (Check sooner to be sure the cheese doesn't burn.) Quickly lift the rounds up with a flexible spatula, and place them over the bottom of a glass or metal can to form a curved shape. Cool and reserve.

MAKES 8 TUILES

FRIED PARSLEY SPRIGS

Frying parsley sprigs adds another look to the garnish, but remember to fry only the leaves, not the stems.

20 to 30 flat-leaf parsley leaves
1 cup vegetable oil for frying
Salt to taste

Wash and dry the parsley leaves; put them into a submersible sieve, and dip them into a tall saucepan with 1 cup of oil heated to 375 degrees. As soon as you hear the hiss of the oil (about 10 to 20 seconds), take them out. If you leave them in longer, they will get soggy. Drain them carefully, then immediately sprinkle them lightly with salt.

MAKES ENOUGH TO GARNISH 4–6 DISHES

FOOD AND WINE EVENTS ARE OFTEN HELD IN THESE RESTORED BUILDINGS AT BECKER VINEYARDS.

APPENDIX

General Information
Texas Department of Agriculture
Web site lists many sources of
produce and artisanal
products.
gotexan.org

Hill Country Fruit Council
(ripening dates, where to buy and
pick your own)
texaspeaches.com

Apples
Love Creek Orchards
Cider Mill and Country Store
P.O. Box 1401, Highway 16
Medina, TX 78055
(800) 449-0882
www.lovecreekorchards.com

Cheese
Fredericksburg Herb Farm (for
herbs and goat cheese)
Bill Varney, Owner
405 Whitney Street
Fredericksburg, TX 78624
(800) 259-4372
www.fredericksburgherbfarm
.com
e-mail: herbfarm@ktc.com

The Mozzarella Company
Paula Lambert, CEO
(214) 741-4072
www.mozzco.com
www.mozzarellacompany.com

Pure Luck Goat Cheese (tours,
festivals, mail order)
www.purelucktexas.com

Greens
Texas Bluebonnet Farms
(210) 865-8623

Lavender
Becker Vineyards (See Wine)

Olive Oil
First Texas Olive Oil Company
Jack Dougherty
Wimberley, TX 78676
(512) 847–6514
www.texasoliveoil.com
e-mail: oliveguy@bvranch.com

Onions
Bell's Farm to Market
McAllen, TX 78501
(800) 798-0424

Texas 1015 Super Sweets
www.sweetonionsource.com

Quail
Diamond H Ranch
5322 Highway 16 North
Bandera, TX 78003
(830) 460-8406
www.texasgourmetquail.com

Ruby Red Grapefruit
For list of shippers, contact:
TexaSweet Citrus Marketing
(956) 580-8004
www.texasweet.com

Strawberries
(see also Oak Hill Farms, below)
Poteet Strawberry Festival
Association
9199 North State Highway 16
Poteet, TX 78065
(888) 742-8144
www.strawberryfestival.com

Tomatoes
Oak Hill Farms
(512) 470-7292

Wine
Becker Vineyards
Bunny and Richard Becker,
Owners
P.O. Box 393
Stonewall, TX 78671
(830) 644-2681
www.beckervineyards.com
e-mail: beckervyds@beecreek.net

Fall Creek Vineyards
Winery: 1820 County Road 222
Tow, TX 78672
(325) 379-5361
Open every day
www.fcv.com
email: info@fcv.com

METRIC CONVERSION TABLES

LIQUID INGREDIENTS

U.S. MEASURES	METRIC	U.S. MEASURES	METRIC
¼ tsp.	1.23 ml	2 Tbsp.	29.57 ml
½ tsp.	2.36 ml	3 Tbsp.	44.36 ml
¾ tsp.	3.70 ml	¼ cup	59.15 ml
1 tsp.	4.93 ml	½ cup	118.30 ml
1 ¼ tsp.	6.16 ml	1 cup	236.59 ml
1 ½ tsp.	7.39 ml	2 cups or 1 pt.	473.18 ml
1 ¾ tsp.	8.63 ml	3 cups	709.77 ml
2 tsp.	9.86 ml	4 cups or 1 qt.	946.36 ml
1 Tbsp.	14.79 ml	4 qts. or 1 gal.	3.79 lt

DRY INGREDIENTS

U.S. MEASURES		METRIC	U.S. MEASURES	METRIC
17 ⅗ oz.	1 livre	500 g	2 oz.	60 (56.6) g
16 oz.	1 lb.	454 g	1 ¾ oz.	50 g
8 ⅞ oz.		250 g	1 oz.	30 (28.3) g
5 ¼ oz.		150 g	⅞ oz.	25 g
4 ½ oz.		125 g	¾ oz.	21 (21.3) g
4 oz.		115 (113.2) g	½ oz.	15 (14.2) g
3 ½ oz.		100 g	¼ oz.	7 (7.1) g
3 oz.		85 (84.9) g	⅛ oz.	3 ½ (3.5) g
2 ⅘ oz.		80 g	¹⁄₁₆ oz.	2 (1.8) g

INDEX

ABOUT THE AUTHORS

Executive Chef **SCOTT COHEN** worked in local restaurants in New Jersey as a teenager and decided to attend the Culinary Institute of America. Upon graduation, his first job was at The Mansion on Turtle Creek in Dallas, where Wolfgang Puck was the corporate chef and Avner Samuelle the executive chef. He then moved to New York City, where he worked as sous chef at The Hotel Carlyle, and later at La Reserve, under the late Andre Gaillard.

With the help of Daniel Boulud, Cohen went to France to do a *stagiaire,* or train with three of that country's most renowned chefs: George Blanc, Roger Verge, and Michel Rustang. He returned to New York to open Tatou, a chic supper club, which garnered him rave reviews. In 1994 he moved to the Stanhope where he transformed the hotel's dining room into an impressive presence on Fifth Avenue. That same year he received the bronze medal from the prestigious Vatel Club, a French culinary organization. He was the youngest chef and one of the first Americans to receive the award.

After sixteen years in New York, Cohen came to San Antonio as executive chef of Las Canarias in the historic landmark hotel La Mansion del Rio. He is also executive chef of its sister restaurant, Pesca on the River in the Watermark Hotel and Spa, just over the footbridge on the other side of the river. Both hotels are part of the Omni hotel system. Under his culinary leadership, Las Canarias has received rave reviews, a AAA four-diamond rating, and was named by Condé Nast as one of the one hundred best restaurants in the world.

Chef Cohen has been showcased at the James Beard House in New York, and was the organizer and host of a James Beard Foundation benefit event in San Antonio featuring the best chefs of that city. He worked with the founder of La Mansion del Rio to launch the San Antonio New World Food and Wine Festival, now in its eighth year. His recipes can be found in **The Food and Wine Cookbook, The Food of Texas: Authentic Recipes from the Lone Star State,** and others. He is on the advisory board of **Chocolatier** and **Pastry Arts** magazines, and is active in many professional and charitable organizations in the culinary world.

MARIAN BETANCOURT is an author and journalist who writes about food for the Associated Press, **Santé** magazine, and other publications. She has written about many well-known chefs, including Daniel Boulud, Bobby Flay, Tom Douglas, Michael Lomonaco, and David Rosengarten. She has published 15 nonfiction books and has written for scores of periodicals. She lives in New York (www.marianbetancourt.com).

RON MANVILLE'S PHOTOGRAPHS are published in many award-winning cookbooks, including the International Association of Culinary Professionals and James Beard award winners, **Sherry Yard's Secrets of Baking** and **Bread Baker's Apprentice.** Other cookbooks include Noel

Cullen's **Elegant Irish Cooking** and Marcel Desaulniers' **Celebrate with Chocolate,** Dwayne Ridgeway's **Lasagna: The Art of Layered Cooking,** and Wolfgang Puck's **Wolfgang Makes It Easy.** Two more books are upcoming. He lives in Rhode Island with his wife, Christine (www.ron manville.com).

ABOUT THE HOTELS AND RESTAURANTS

Omni's **LA MANSION DEL RIO** and its sister organization, the **WATERMARK HOTEL AND SPA,** are located across from each other on the famed River Walk of San Antonio. Since it opened in 1968, La Mansion del Rio has hosted hundreds of celebrities, from President Bill Clinton to the prince of Morocco, not to mention legions of film and entertainment celebrities. La Mansion del Rio is in a former nineteenth-century school. It is now a historic landmark building that reflects the city's Spanish Colonial heritage, with its graceful arches and columns, cloistered courtyards, and romantic interiors. Las Canarias is named for the early settlers from the Canary Islands. Its old world charm comes through in the modern Provençal haute cuisine that is meticulously presented. It was rated the best restaurant on San Antonio's River Walk the year it opened.

The Watermark Hotel and Spa opened in 2004 and immediately earned the Mobil Four Star Award, one of only two hotels in Texas to receive this distinction. It also garnered the Condé Nast **Traveler** gold list rating as one of the top 100 hotels in the world and in 2006 it was voted number one. Its restaurant, Pesca on the River, equally as elegant as Las Canarias, is more modern and casual. **Texas Monthly** magazine rated it one of the best restaurants in Texas the year it opened.

Some of the signature dishes from both restaurants are included in this book.